Flight Patterns

A Poetry Collection

Flight Patterns

A Poetry Collection

by

Mary K O'Melveny

© 2023 Mary K O'Melveny. All rights reserved.
This material may not be reproduced in any form, published,
reprinted, recorded, performed, broadcast,
rewritten or redistributed without
the explicit permission of Mary K O'Melveny.
All such actions are strictly prohibited by law.

Cover photo by Anne W. Hornsby—ahornsbyimages.com
Cover design input by Elizabeth Anastasia O'Melveny
Cover design by Shay Culligan

ISBN: 978-1-63980-370-5

Kelsay Books
502 South 1040 East, A-119
American Fork, Utah 84003
Kelsaybooks.com

More praise for *Flight Patterns*

Through clarity of her skillful imagery, Mary creates lasting poetic moments of gratitude, love and awakening. She gives voice to personal and global losses, and gives us wings to cope with the weight, height, depth, distance of existence. It's a stunning modern book of awareness!

—Jerrice J. Baptiste, Author, Poetry Facilitator, Host, *WKZE Women of Note*

"What kind of people write about birds?" asks the title of one poem in Mary O'Melveny's new collection Flight Patterns. The rest of the book provides an answer to that question, in the process revealing that while birds (and other winged things) do appear throughout, she's really not writing about them so much as what they have always represented to us land-bound humans: the freedom of flight, and of flight in all of its meanings, of movement, escape, transition, even death. For as she writes elsewhere here, "a poem is never / just about its subject matter. /Metaphor matters as much as / lyrical style. . . ." Her metaphorical birds populate a lyrical sky, offering wisdom and hope (and an occasional mouse). But she also writes of how birds are disappearing from the literal sky, "Empty limbs as epilogue." As a labor rights advocate turned poet, her passion for justice informs her verse, compelling her readers to examine the world from which we would take flight—and to imagine the place where we might wish to alight.

—Larry W. Moore, publisher, Broadstone Books

A lovely, ambitious, timely work. The poet invites the reader into the world of birdwatching and beyond where we encounter birds in an entirely unique and contagious light. This collection is filled with movement. From the vivid detail of lives lost to COVID in "Lost Dreamers," to the quirky flight patterns recounted in poems such as "Anthropomorphizing." "Elegy For A Queen," "Night Witches" and "Escape Velocity," the author takes us on journeys as surprising as they are new.

—Charlotte Pence, Author *CODE, Many Small Fires*

Fulvous Tree Duck

Drawing by Bess O'Melveny MacMaugh

Acknowledgments

Thanks to the editors and readers of these publications where these poems first saw the light of day:

Allegro Poetry Magazine: "Murmurations"

Beltway Poetry Quarterly: "Why Do People Write About Birds," "Quantum Entanglements"

Chronogram: "Who Can Hear A Love Song?"

Coastal Shelf Magazine: "Mourning Our Dead" (revised)

From Roars To Whispers (Quarantine Tales Issue 7): "Flight. Reimagined"

Into The Void: "Perseid Meteor Showers"

Jerry Jazz Musician: "How To Write a Poem About A Woodpecker," "If I Were A Monarch Butterfly"

Jewish Currents: "Cease Fire" (Raynes Poetry Competition Winner 2017)

Junto Magazine: "sounds of music when birds have left us" first appeared as Part IV of the poem "Reverberations"

Lightwood Literary Magazine: "Ode To Companionship

The New Verse News: "A Monarch Butterfly Poses Some Questions," "Re-Thinking Basic Dance Steps," "International Women's Day 2022," "Cloud Cover," "What Is the Definition of Exodus?"

Sleet: The Inside Edition II: "Mourning Our Dead"

Science Write Now: "How I Learned To Fly Like A Cat"

The Wolff Literary Magazine: "Game Theory"

The Write Place at the Write Time: "The Reincarnation Of Flight," "To Be Blessed"

Writing In A Woman's Voice: "Stork Stories"

Anthologies and Collections

American Writers Review (San Fedele Press, 2021): "What Is a Dream After All?" "Hope In The Unseen"

American Writers Review (San Fedele Press, 2022): "Confessions Of A Casual Birdwatcher," "The End of Civilization"

A Woman of a Certain Age (Finishing Line Press, 2018): "Fireflies," "Bird Sanctuary"

An Apple In Her Hand (Codhill Books, 2019): "Love Nest"

Breaking The Ground Rules (Mediacs Books, 2022): "Artemis On A Wild Hunt," "Grey Is More Than Color's Absence: A Haibun," "Lost Dreamers," "Journal Entry: Great Horned Owl"

Dispatches From The Memory Care Museum (Kelsay Books, 2021): "Observing The Passage Of Venus"

Merging Star Hypotheses (Finishing Line Press, 2020): "Escape Velocity"

Personal Appreciations

While almost everyone is fascinated by the idea of flight, it became near-obsessional as fear of COVID-19 forced us all indoors, behind masks, isolated from society's "normal" give and take. For far too long, most of my personal contact, apart from my wife Susan and close family members, consisted of tiny computer squares at Zoom meetings or involved creatures from the natural world, especially the many wild birds who surround our home near Woodstock, New York. As any bird-lover knows, birds offer both unending entertainment and valuable lessons in adaptability and optimism. I am grateful to the nesting pair of bald eagles who have made their home at the edge of our woods for many years. When I feel a bit lost or disheartened by the sorry state of the universe, even a brief sighting of those eagles is magical and restorative.

The pandemic "pause" did allow time for generous editorial input from dear friends as this volume progressed. Mary Gawronski read various versions and offered helpful feedback on many of the works included here. This collection was also strengthened by insightful commentary from acclaimed poet Rhina P. Espaillat and by edits from literature professor Charlotte Pence. Some of the poems included here got their start in workshops helmed by the gracious, talented poet Jerrice J. Baptiste; others received input from my friends Tana Miller, Jan Zlotnik-Schmidt, Eileen Howard and Kappa Waugh, all members of the Hudson Valley Women's Writing Group.

Finally, I am grateful for ongoing help from my sister, Elizabeth A. O'Melveny, artist and website creator, and to my grandmother, Bess O'Melveny MacMaugh. Bess was far ahead of her time in building an artistic career during the 1940s and 1950s at the U.S. Department of the Interior and the Smithsonian Museum. Her beautiful pen and ink drawings inspired my first appreciation for the many species of birds that infuse our planet with hope, light and optimism.

Contents

Part I: Flight Patterns

A Late October Convocation	21
My First Lesson In Flight Patterns	23
A Monarch Butterfly Poses Some Questions*	24
Chrysalis	25
Stork Stories	26
Fireflies	27
Elegy For A Queen	28
Red Doorways	29
Gray Is More Than Color's Absence: A Haibun	30
Tangerine Honeycreepers At The Medical Lab	31
Miracle Of The Honeybees*	32
Night Witches*	33
Game Theory	35
Perseid Meteor Showers	37
Trying On The Wings Of Prayer*	38
Artemis On A Wild Hunt	39
There Will Be No Swan Song	41
International Women's Day	42
How To Come To Terms With Airborne Dangers	43
Is Exodus The Same As Flight?*	45
Do You Know How To Define Freedom?	47
Escape Velocity*	48
Saying Goodbye To Lawrence Ferlinghetti	53
Building Castles In The Sky	55
Lost Dreamers	56

Part II: Birdwatching/Birds Watching

What Kind Of People Write About Birds?	61
Love Nest	62
A Pre-COVID Bus Ride	64
Bird Sanctuary	65

The Reincarnation Of Flight	66
Savoring Winter's Silences	67
Bird Watcher's Diary*	68
Murmurations*	69
An Ordinary Day*	70
Transformations	71
Couples Counseling Advice From Great Horned Owls*	72
Examining The Heart Of The Matter	73
Countercurrents	74
How To Write A Woodpecker Poem	76
What Do Old Birds Talk About?	79
Anthropomorphizing	80
Confessions Of A Casual Bird Watcher	81
Mourning Dove Portfolios	82
Flightless Birds	83
Journal Entry: Great Horned Owl	85
Winter Navigation Lessons	86
Mourning Our Dead	87
In The Wind. I*	88
Quantum Entanglements	89
How To Tally Some Of Our Abundant Losses*	90
La Clairvoyance*	92
Creating The Sounds Of Music*	93
Who Can Hear A Love Song?*	95
Sounds of music when birds have left us	96

Part III: Flight. Reimagined

Man Talking To Bird*	99
The Future Of Civilization*	100
If I Were A Monarch Butterfly	102
To Be Blessed	103
Flight. Reimagined. I	104

In The Beginning Was The Fear	105
Re-Thinking Basic Dance Steps	106
what is a dream after all	107
Cease Fire*	108
The Languages We Need To Hear	109
How I Learned To Fly Like A Cat	111
Is There A Cure For Sadness?	112
Observing The Passage Of Venus	113
Ode To Companionship	114
Hope In The Unseen	115
Exploring The Limits Of Curiosity	116
In The Wind. II	117
When Hope Is The Thing We Want To Convey*	118
A Brief History Of Optimism	119
What It Might Mean To Catch A Passing Asteroid	121
Cloud Cover*	123
Villanelle For Black Holes*	125
Infinity's Memoirs: As Told By The James Webb Telescope	126
Tales From a Weather Balloon	128
Examining Images From Space Telescopes	129
Sestina For Light Dreams	131
Flight. Reimagined. II*	133

* Notes on Selected Poems

Poems in this volume whose title is followed by an asterisk have a backstory referenced in the Notes section following the final poem on page 133.

*I pray to the birds because they remind me
of what I love rather than what I fear.
And at the end of my prayers,
they teach me how to listen.*

—Terry Tempest Williams,
Refuge: An Unnatural History of Family and Place

Part I:

Flight Patterns

Nothing happens until something moves.
—Albert Einstein

On paper, a butterfly never dies.
—Jacqueline Woodson, *Brown Girl Dreaming*

A Late October Convocation

I catch the pattern of your silence before you speak
—Langston Hughes

My mother and I stand in stillness, just as clouds
flame russet, peach, lavender. Snow geese arc
over a Delaware wildlife sanctuary's pale waters
like a convocation of wimpled nuns or ivory-robed
monks assembling for evening vespers.

As patterns of movement reflect against liquid
surface, it looks like thousands of worshippers
have gathered to bid the sun a final farewell
or gently applaud a still-shy moon as it takes
its tentative steps toward horizon's apse.

My mother reaches for my hand while we watch
the watershed shape-shift like diamond-crocheted
linen threads. I think of our lace-making Irish
ancestors whose needles fluttered to knot each
intricate rosette, shamrock, curved vine, tiny bird

before their work sailed off to grace christening gowns
and bridal dresses of European aristocrats or the sleeves
or hems of priests whose vestments glinted with early
convent light. Multitudes of white geese glide, sweep,
bow like celebrants joining a religious procession.

Wings flutter like flower petals unleashed by late-day
winds or ruffled tutus of dance troupes at dress rehearsal.
They float, rise, swoon, soar above tiny pink shells,
tan-striped mollusks, largemouth bass, white perch.
We are all as hushed as penitents awaiting forgiveness.

Barely six months later, my mother is dead. Our sanctuary trip was among the last serene moments of our own long migration. Now, that same silence emerges from space telescope visions of cinnamon rose-hued clouds, crystal-studded dust, star-stacked galaxies—our final shared language.

My First Lesson In Flight Patterns

I was eight when I grew my first wings.
My family had gone for a weekend hike
at the base of Mount Rainer. My father,
tall as an evergreen, lay down on the ground
to teach my baby sister and me how to make
snow angels. Instead of shouting as usual,
he was calm. Focused on rhythm, movement.
We began slowly, as we flapped our arms
back and forth in frothy frostings of white,
then sped up as we moved toward escape velocity.

In my dream later, we rose like great egrets
en route from Maine to California by way of
Florida, clocking in at fifty miles per hour.
Our ornamental plumes fanned out behind us
like kites made from hand-stitched lace-webbed
wedding veils. We soared above craggy peaks,
cornrowed treetops, crisscrossed wheatfields,
stared at deserts abloom in mauve, yellow, crimson,
landed briefly at ponds and marshlands filled with frogs,
crayfish, dragonflies who had not invited us to dine.

Taking flight from our whitened landing pad
felt like a miracle. A first vision of what might
be possible on the strength of desire alone.
My sister's snowsuit was palest sky blue,
like an egret's egg, stark against a milky ground.
A hush descended, as if everyone had vanished
into morning air like memories of campfire smoke.
Elevation became us all. Even my angry father,
now transformed to choreographer, was saintly.
Who could ever know our lives? Now that we could fly.

A Monarch Butterfly Poses Some Questions*

Do you remember the noise of my wings?
A lace veil as it flirts with a summer breeze.
A blade of grass as it shakes off morning dew.

In Mexico, a million of us sound like waterfalls.
At rest, we cling to tree limbs like gold, onyx,
ivory jewelry that has been hidden from thieves.

We fly high above sleeping migrants everywhere,
whose hopes pirouette in zephyrs and exospheres
as they dream of flight patterns to safety.

Do you recall the first time you saw one of us?
How you were awed by our delicate wings, how
we landed like a first kiss on a purple cone flower?

How you imagined what it would be like to float,
unfettered, without apology? Without accountability?
How it takes so little to ignite imagination's fiery call.

Our journeys from your garden to jungle sanctuaries
span generations. Some days the ground is littered
with scales that resemble coins from Spanish galleons.

I have been airborne for 2,500 miles. I have traversed
obstacles my ancestors never knew: poisoned fields,
droughts, drones and planes, wildfires, clearcut forests.

Still, think of that moment of lift, when air currents
lick your skin as a lover might. Always optimists,
we remain your ardent guides to Elysian Fields.

Chrysalis

This was going to be a poem
about hope's power. Of emergence
from weeks in sheltered spaces,
transformed to newer selves.

Healed, our imaginations ran wild.
Our shells turned rainbow-hued,
translucent scales unfolded, stretched.
Lifted from retreat, how we soared.

But I am writing from my tent
in Idlib, Syria. Shared by
three families, our cocoons are
cobalt blue sheets of thin plastic.

Prayers are as fragile here as
butterflies. Once I saw a False
Apollo resting on a rock.
Its wings were black and white, dots

of royal blue, eye spots of russet.
I tried to imagine how it might
mimic its mythic namesake.
How it might soar like a poem.

Stork Stories

for Oona and Esme

My godchild has given birth to a baby
girl, her second child. The birth was
smooth and relatively swift. Kate's
own birth took much longer than a day.
We were all so young when we gathered
to celebrate beside the stone fireplace in my
Woodstock living room. We bore poems,
feathers, crystals and champagne. We were
filled with moral certainties, predictions for
our lives based on little more than nerve.

I find it is impossible not to think of storks.
those legendary bearers of good tidings, luck,
who transport the newly hatched in their wide
beaks. Old legends say babies will come
if sweet treats are left to rest on windowsills.
In Spain, nesting pairs of white storks fill up
rooftops. They sweep and glide through skies
like seasoned flamenco dancers, their calls
to mate reverberating like castanets.

Each year, these storks migrate from Spain
to Africa and back. In one day, they can
travel four hundred kilometers. They leave
behind sun-drenched Savannahs, sweep past
the Black Sea, the Bosporus Straits, sail
on warm winds until they reach a roost they
knew before. This is my wish for both great
goddaughters—to catch each updraft,
free-wheel as wetlands mirror a sunrise,
always trusting there is a safe landing spot.

Fireflies

for Baylor and Cameron

Twilight drifts down
like a lazy curtain.
Legos and shiny spacecraft
lie scattered around the room,
tiny plastic truck parts mixed
in with battle gear, racquets, balls.
Our nephews' attention spans wane
as computer games are powered down.
Skeptical looks meet our tales
of soon-to-be magical sightings.

Suddenly, an impetuous twinkle
like wild lightening winks beside
a bush. Eyes widen as another
arrives. Then another. Our yard
has come alive with bioluminescence.
We can almost hear thunderbolts
as stars land on the grass
like a rare moment of truth.
Our nephews race outside,
breathless, dizzy with excitement.

In an instant, tiny winged insects
have overpowered Toys R Us gear.
Our eager young chasers, jars in hand,
squeal in delight as flickering yellows,
pale greens sprout in the air where they
float, flicker just past their reach.
Suddenly, we recall our own summers
of long ago, as if we had just walked indoors,
the thrill of sparkling night air
still rising and falling in our chests.

Elegy For A Queen

her nest is round as a soccer ball
a bald-faced hornet queen
chewed and spit and wrapped
it tight like an ancient bookbinder
she stashed her eggs in combs
tucked it inside a golden maple
a man in a space suit holds
her papery world in his hands

we hated to bring it down
but a hornet's sting is vicious
their anger is righteous
no choice but to send troops
soon enough we will forget
why we were so upset
the maple leaves will slip away
next year's queen will wake

Red Doorways

A great-great grandfather's Antrim
doorway was likely cherry-colored
to spite the Brits who demanded
black to celebrate Victoria's reign.

Scottish ancestors were said to paint
their doorways claret once they paid
off the mortgage. A celebration
of freedom from red ink burdens.

In my dream, our newly painted
door has flickered its *Welcome*
like an underground railroad stop.
In dark night, its amber glow shimmers.

An émigré emerges from the forest,
bent like a runaway sensing heat.
She pushes past worries that white
clouds of breath will reveal her form.

The black bear lumbers toward me.
She has eaten all our apples as Fall's leaves
have begun to slip, turn russet, ruddy, blood-speckled.
Your red door called me she whispers.

Gray Is More Than Color's Absence: A Haibun

First strands of pearled gray likely settled down into my hair like ash twenty-five years ago as I stared at my office telephone one afternoon. *It's malignant* said the disembodied male voice on the line (in the same timbre that had assured me through test after test that there was no cause for worry). His words swept over me like wind-blown first frost. I walked down the hallway to see if the third eye of fright painted on my forehead was visible to others but no one looked up. Over the course of weeks, months, each lock of my hair turned pale as a slant of light on early snow. Over the years, some asked (often in slightly hushed tones) if I had considered "coloring" my hair—*to make you look younger.* But I understood that each fine, moonshine filament was a rogue cell banished, a fear dispatched. The way water birds suddenly rise up from the sea in a cloud before disappearing into a dusky sky. I was steeled toward survival instead of loss.

> Shadows can haunt us
> or gift us with lambent light
> to cloak our worst fears

Tangerine Honeycreepers At The Medical Lab

It is steamy and hot.
Our skin sheds teardrops
of sweat, our hair frizzes.
Crimson anthuriums
shaped like valentine hearts
glisten beneath shiny green vines,
each yellow and white spadix
wagging like a gossipy tongue.
Nearby, birds of paradise
emerge from the bent ends
of their long greenish stalks.
Their bright orange floral fans,
tufted with royal blue,
look ready to soar, as if
they were tangerine honeycreepers
about to burst into song before
they sail off into a cerulean sky.
A flock of rose-ringed parakeets
peek out from behind Royal
Palm fronds. Whitecapped waves
breathe in and out above a turquoise
sea, kicking a coconut back
and forth like a soccer ball.
We wrap ourselves in smooth
sound ribbons of slack key
guitars that shimmer as sun sets.
There are no icicles. No snow or sleet.
No broken trees or frozen pipes.
No fractured limbs or vanished power.
There is no infusion room
where veins fill with dubious
cell-killing fluids. Deep in this jungle,
all is calm. Serene. Revelatory.

Miracle Of The Honeybees*

A volcano spit its innards
into skies emptied of birds.

An island became a scarred field,
sordid as a crematorium.

Inevitably, the sun rose
to expose smoldering carnage.

I am the village beekeeper,
returned to assess fates and failures.

My hives lie scattered like war debris
along this charcoaled landscape.

I had hoped these bees might outfly
the raining fire, swarm past death.

As I sit down on the grainy ash
to mourn my losses, a sound takes shape.

A throbbing heartbeat, insistent,
like a marching band's vibrations.

My bees have saved themselves from famine,
from misfortune's fiasco end.

Like architects, they recast their chambered
hives as new habitats, with grit and glue-like resin.

They gorged on combs of honey to seal
themselves away from calamity.

I stare, spellbound by honeybee wisdom,
as my apian companions welcome me home.

Night Witches*

These sorcerers
slipped past skeptics
like stealth shadows.
A platoon of
Russian women
flew night sorties.
Nazis feared them,
called them
hags and vixens.
Their aged bi-planes—
worn wooden crop
dusters—carried
no radios
no parachutes
no guns or radar.
Their gear was
maps, stopwatches,
flashlights. On their
own in frozen
darkness, frostbite
turned their hands white
as if old ghosts
were bearing down
on each target,
the glide down smooth
as a gauzy
scarf adrift on
a summer breeze.

They traveled in
packs. First one was
the bait, hustling
for targets. Last
one in, engines
idling, dispatched

the bombs *swoosh swoosh*
As daylight neared,
they disembarked,
undressed from their
castoff clothing,
removed stuffing
from hand-me-down
boots, shouted out
successful kills,
mourned lost sisters.
Afterwards, they
brushed their hair, picked
up their knitting
needles, painted
yellow flowers
on their airplanes,
put on lipstick,
danced like show girls.

Game Theory

sun seared the afternoon
erased memories of rain
I had just opened the porch door
stepped onto the deck
when I saw her
a black bear   much bigger than me
climbing up our ancient apple tree

just like last week
up   up   up
last time she bounced
so far out on one limb
it swayed like wheat in a windstorm
apples poured down on the lawn
she came back for them later
today she and I stared at each other
directly   as neighbors might

bears can see as well as humans
despite myths to the contrary
I would swear she knew
I was trying to decide
if I should go back inside
for my camera phone   or safety
we both hesitated

it was the *whack* of the door
that startled her   sent her scrambling
back down the trunk
though she was in no hurry
at the bottom she stopped   looked up
still eyeing those apples overhead
I could almost see her shrug

before she loped off
headed for the meadow
every few feet she stopped
looked back
as if trying to decide
whether to venture a return
for a few more bites

choices were waiting to be made
I   inside   camera on the table
she   tree   apples on the branch
each of us
waiting
watching
wondering
what are risks worth taking

Perseid Meteor Showers

Sitting on the porch deck
in obscure night darkness,
I am searching the sky
for signs of shooting stars

while thinking deep sea
burials. Perseus,
grandson of Zeus,
adrift, floating to Seriphos.

Mother and son released,
dark oracle prophesies
submerged, the hero god's
trajectories begin.

Gorgon, sea monsters slain.
Pegasus born of their blood.
Andromeda rescued.
Athena victorious.

Yet, despite all, rescue
proves inadequate. He
cannot be saved from fate.
His great star flares, then falls.

Trying On The Wings Of Prayer*

the unarmed man stood by himself
in his grandmother's yard
talking on his cell phone

police deaths keep on stealing children
when we implore *for god's sake why*
they tell us all to pray

does anyone think prayers will elevate
our sorrows   instead we are plummeting
like Icarus in the sun

you might see us sail   over street corners
past yards highways   storefronts playgrounds
cop stops   classrooms   park benches

we are floating around like blackbirds
don't forget to ask *for god's sake why*
so far nobody answers this question

we search for cover   for meaning
our pleas drift   slip through our fingers   unspool
we spiral downward   into the sea

from our lofty prayer perch
we can still observe tearful families
hear lame excuses rain down like melting wax

cops keep on killing   bodies keep on crashing
imprecations fail us   broken wings   stolen grace
for god's sake why   can't we stop it

Artemis On A Wild Hunt

The night sky is a wolf's mouth today and Artemis,
bathed in solitude, is on her wild hunt.
—Nikita Gill

NASA may finally send a woman
to the moon. Artemis will carry new
explorers in search of life sources
that may have been missed by Armstrong, Aldrich,
Collins or those who followed along for a
few years until we decided there was
nothing much to see but dusty
boot prints and a hastily planted flag.

Artemis, daughter of Zeus and Leto,
sister of Apollo, must have laughed out loud
when all the men piled into her
brother's namesake voyager. She is,
after all, goddess of the Moon, the hunt,
all that is wild and unknown. He, god of
poetry, song and dance, far better
suited to calming earthly unease.

What might Artemis be seeking on
hidden icy corners of the Moon's south
pole, concealed from our earthly view?
Its crepuscular surface is tightly sheathed,
virginal. Maybe that's the point.
Unspoiled. Unseen. Untouched. Not like
our burning, drowning planet, soiled from end
to end with Styrofoam cups and cigarette butts.

There are no stags, hawks, boars
or hunting dogs to be discovered
on the moon's stygian soil.
And soon, no more on earth.

And so, as fires consume us, it must be
that Artemis hunts for ice. She raises
her golden bow. Her arrows fly
toward an umbra of waning light.

There Will Be No Swan Song

> *I will play the swan, / And die in music.*
> —Emilia, *Othello,* Act 5, Scene 2.

Some say Ukraine's national bird
is a brash, bold swan. She is long-necked,
heavy breasted, with a ten-foot wingspan,
legs that dangle like colored charcoal sticks.
Cygnets are best known for coy romance,
loyalty, grace. Their intertwined heart-shaped
forms call to us of lyrical chorales, of lovers.
Some prefer to watch them as they glide
like nursery rhymes beneath a golden
yellow sun over cornflower blue lakes.
Swans are fierce in territorial defense,
do not waste time on tuneful vocalizing.
They are mostly white, though some sport
black feathers, as if singed while they soared
above mortal lives or bombed out buildings.

Putin, playing Zeus, thought to co-opt
the bird for his own—a swift deflowering
in winter's stealthy silence. Leda sees
through his charade, knows such brazen lust
will not succeed. Garbed in swan feathers
of her own, she twirls, leans, begs, bows,
bites. She faces off, fights like a fury against all odds.
Socrates believed some flute-like swan's death wail
foretold joy. Less so Cassandra, facing Agamemnon
as his prize of war. In these more modern times,
the sound you hear is Leda as she hisses and spits,
her eight-foot wingspan roiling chilled air,
scapulars crushed, humerals snapped, necks broken.
She will not die. Will not sing farewell.

International Women's Day

Today, please celebrate all
the women we have lost.
In every war and cease fire.
On slaver's ships. On thirsty
desert treks to walled borders.
In back-alley rooms without
anesthesia. Locked in basements,
without papers or escape routes.
Asleep in bed. Hitching a ride.
Nursing bruises or starving babies.

Our losses rise like mountain peaks.
Ukrainian women huddle in subways,
clutch children, family pets, a few
hastily gathered objects from lives
they will likely never know again
or tattered photographs of loved ones
who may be lost forever. Even in
safer worlds, friends die of causes
that repurposed money, refocused
attention could have remedied.

Some fade away from neglect,
inattention, dreams downsized
by school guidance counselors,
religious zealots, patriarchy.
Others drop dead without a whimper
on a sun-dappled afternoon. One friend's
memories vanished by midnight
stroke; another's by subtle daily
erasures. Open our mouths wide in
praise of all. Let songbirds loose.

How To Come To Terms With Airborne Dangers

A Cooper Hawk soars overhead, its prey
an orange-throated thrush practicing notes
like an opera star. As silken sound spills,
turns quiet as a snowdrift, a bank of clouds
shifts position, dances across ashen skies
as if this day might yet be cause for joy.

Haven't we all had days where we thought joy
was on our calendar? Before we fell prey
to someone else's ideas about our life. Skies,
once bright with wish-willed dreams, turned to inked notes
of foreboding. In such moments, regret clouds
our thinking. Our desires are dimmed by spills

of waterfall tears. Even when we want to spill
out our anguished thoughts, replace them with joy,
cruel fate steps in our way as shadow clouds
our cosmos. Humans, like songbirds, can fall prey
to unseen dangers. We scan ground, fieldnotes
in hand, look down, not up at clear blue skies.

Syrians know well how death rains from skies
as well as land. Drones, missiles, rockets spill
flames from every angle. As bodies mount, notes
of war's victims cannot keep pace. No joy
comes easily. Some days, that concept preys
on a war's victims—its memory clouds

their vision like a cataract. Once clouds
meant not ruin but ghazals written to skies
by avian poets. A farmer's crops fall prey
to rust, water, heat. Soldiers' boots now spill
across wheatfields, crushing ripe kernels. Joy
of harvests replaced by bankruptcy's notes.

Our warming climate sounds these same dire notes.
A shrinking ozone layer burns away clouds.
We stand exposed beneath a sun, once joy-
ous guardian, now avenging angel. Skies
grant no more grace to wistful dreamers, but spill
thunder doom warnings. Everything is prey.

We are left to seek joy in each moment, to take notes
before memory clouds, falls prey to passing hawks
as they emerge from brightest skies. Before hope spills.

Is Exodus The Same As Flight?*

Before I fall asleep each night,
I stare up at my curvaceous ceiling,
darkened by age, pock-marked
by stone, spider webs, jagged roots.

Each "room" is bordered by rock slabs,
boulders, dirt mounds. My clay cook
pots sit behind me. To the right, my sleep
ledge is softened by keffiyehs, quilts.

I have swept one center section
almost flat. An aid worker found us
a wooden table with two crooked
shelves. My prayer rug is folded there.

In that corner to the left, a brass box
still holds my yellowed deed to this land.
Tanks have bulldozed my three homes.
Now my sheep graze overhead.

These crooked steps, long smoothed by water,
footfalls, wind downward from their pen.
That slim cord dangling above provides
just enough light to read Fadwa Tuqan.

Like me, most of my neighbors have burrowed
beneath West bank hillsides we once owned.
Above ground, apricots, almonds, olives
thrive, as they have since Ottoman times.

Jurists who know nothing of our narratives
have ruled that we must evacuate, as if
we were as nomadic as our grazing flocks.
They name us trespassers, transients.

The army says our villages are best
suited as live-fire training grounds.
No one wants neighbors who remember
every whisper of their past lives.

I still have the dented bronzed key
to our ancestral dwelling place.
In chilled night air, I am warmed
by memory's refracted light.

Do You Know How To Define Freedom?

Ask any random gazelle what it is
and she will tell you to measure the space
between her and the lion in pursuit.

Ask Janis and she will tell you, in her
graveled voice, about what may remain
in place once someone clears away the rubble.

Ask a migrant and she will tell you she feels
like a monarch butterfly whose flight pushed
through category five hurricane winds.

Ask a great blue heron and she will tell you
how she can soar lean and low above a creek
and hear the songs of rainbow trout and frogs.

Ask any woman who clung to some man's
whispered promises like a trapeze bar and she
will tell you a story about *Roe v. Wade*.

Escape Velocity*

I.

shouldn't we be
plotting our grand
getaways   night
often works best
though daybreak can
sometimes provide
cover   one blends
in with rush of
crowds on their way
to purposeful
tasks   energy's din
for company

my mother sat
for day after day
at a small town
bus depot   she
meant to pass her
cash to the clerk
dreamt of how far
it might take her
lacking luggage
or IOUs
tried to picture
her light new life

how hard it is
to stay tethered
once freedom tempts
we begin to
stare hard at
windows   measure

doorways   rooftops
calculate weight
height   depth   distance
keep mind journals
which cannot be
used against us

we crawl through
mangrove forests
cypress swamplands
guided only
by distant stars
and drinking gourds
songs of freedom
propel us toward
some distant point
where we conjure
our unfettered
new world visions

II.

our sad planet
sinks   dries   burns up
cyclone winds roar
dry land recedes
pollinators gone
prayers fill fields
in one eye blink
skies go silent
some days I am
tempted to ask
god about an
afterlife

maybe she can
spare some
jobless angel
lazy or kind
skilled at
explanations
maybe I will
feel prepared
with a backbeat
of winged voices
to aid us as
we abscond

elevations tempt us
to steal away
go higher than
we ever have
safer perhaps
or just different
we'll don space suits
head for the stars
we'll wave goodbye
travel weightless
all the way to
Venus or Mars

III.

I have always
loved Houdini
how he managed
disappearance
as if he just

slipped on some
dinner jacket
or elegant
Harry Blackstone
who could send a
caged canary
to another sphere
or levitate
a princess from
her fainting couch

once my father
took me to watch
Mr. Blackstone
float a lightbulb
in a darkened
theatre as we
followed its arc
as if possessed
dreaming of the ride

the *idea* was
the magic
breaking away
from gravity's
pull   leaning in
to places no
one had measured
or predicted
to spaces where
dimensions might
not be confined
to only three

when I grew up
women did not
pilot airplanes
or lead space missions
they were *practical*
down to earth
nurtured by nature
they *stayed put* even
when ground caved in
no wonder so many
of us choose
to fly away

Saying Goodbye To Lawrence Ferlinghetti

Lawrence Ferlinghetti lived much longer
than my college friend Page who sat
with me in empty classrooms
memorizing *A Coney Island of the Mind.*

We dressed up all in black
from felt berets to cotton stockings.
I had bongo drums. In case someone
missed the point about the Beats.

We imagined our lives on the road,
How we would howl at injustice
as we circled the globe in an old
Hudson, how we would sit at our Royal

typewriters where words would tumble
out like flocks of sparrows and everyone
would envy us, admiring how we tossed
conventions away like so many breadcrumbs.

We imagined faces rapt with attention
on uncomfortable stools in some dingy
West Village club while we proved hip,
spoke of *moonmad swans* and *falcons of the inner eye.*

Soon we would be off to City Lights
where our own words would stop a show cold,
goose bumps forming on every arm, because
we would be acrobats, just like him, willing

to leap into the unknown just for the sake
of the dare, of absurdity's constant risk.
Oh how we wanted to fly!
Back then, we never looked down.

Page died of breast cancer when
Ferlinghetti was as young as I am now.
I see the three of us, garbed in youthful fantasies,
writing our autobiographies anew.

Building Castles In The Sky

Falling is the consequence that we accept
for our decision to leave the ground.
—Lor Saborn, Flagstaff, AZ professional rock climber, quoted in
The New York Times Magazine, July 25, 2021

Some days, dreams race down the runways
of our mind like jumbo Boeings
packed with backstories and wishful thinking.
Thrill of speed, lift of air, hitch of breath
as plane rises from ground to space.
We follow its trajectory, cross fingers
as bustling commerce transmutes
to crazy quilt geometric patterns, streaks of hazy light.
In that brief silence, known boundaries merge.
We become architects, engineers, exhale as clouds
form blueprints beneath our windowed stares.
Once airborne, we see that flight is just
a first conceit. Gravity waits.

Lost Dreamers

*Hold fast to dreams/For if dreams die/Life is a broken-winged bird/
That cannot fly.*
                            —Langston Hughes, "Dreams"

More than one million dead.
The ground is littered with feathers.

A shot glass resting at bar's edge.
A Yankees cap nesting on a coat rack.

A stethoscope stashed in a pocket.
A cell phone encased in a plastic bag.

A dog-eared book of Whitman.
An underlined Introduction to Chemistry.

An unopened collection notice.
An email returned by the daemon mailer.

An I Heart Grandma sweatshirt.
A Best Dad Ever coffee mug.

A Social Studies teacher's manual.
A pair of yellow rubber cleaning gloves.

A thermoplastic blue construction hard hat.
An antique Freshwater pearl necklace.

A citizenship exam study guide.
A Valentine, unopened on an oak desk.

A well-worn red plaid wool flannel shirt.
A pair of lightly scuffed Air Jordans.

A half-used jar of Pond's cold cream.
A half-drunk bottle of Jack Daniels.

A blackthorn Shillelagh with a copper tip.
A sauce-stained white linen chef's apron.

A beige wool cardigan sweater with a missing button.
A black silk dress with spaghetti straps, unworn for years.

A spruce-topped Alhambra Flamenco guitar.
A synthetic leather black and white soccer ball.

A Navajo wedding basket.
A Kente cloth dashiki, size XXXL.

A just-opened jar of Vaseline.
A dusty bottle of Old Spice.

A DVD of The Great American Songbook.
A floral tin index box of family recipes.

A still-open checkerboard on a coffee table.
A slightly rusted set of garden tools by the steps.

A red and white cotton Kaffiyeh.
A pair of 2.5 Readers with a tortoise shell frame.

A carved bamboo Quran holder.
A Naugahyde Book of Common Prayer.

A sepia-tinted wedding photograph.
A bronzed baby shoe.

A vintage denim jacket with copper studs.
A paperback copy of The Autobiography of Malcom X.

An original vinyl recording of Sketches of Spain.
A St. Jude rosary made of turquoise beads, blessed by Pope Francis.

A bright blue six-foot nylon dog leash.
An empty white wire bird cage.

*When this poem was first written in 2022, 100,000 people in the United States had succumbed to COVID-19. By March 1, 2023, nearly 1,118,000 had died from the disease.

Part II:

Birdwatching/Birds Watching

If you want to see birds, you must have birds in your heart.
—John Burroughs

What Kind Of People Write About Birds?

> *Colonizers write about flowers.*
> *I tell you about children throwing rocks*
> *at Israeli tanks seconds before becoming daisies.*
>   —Noor Hindi, *Fuck Your Lecture on Craft, My People Are Dying*

I love to write about birds. What might this mean?
White skin privilege? Classism? Failure of nerve?
Cluelessness about those marathon human tragedies
circling our globe like murders of crows?
Some days everything is cause for weeping.
Our grass is filled with great lakes of water.

Our purple martin house lists in the meadow,
pushed aslant by frozen ground.
Will it right itself by April or tumble
over like a fallen idol? Its prospective
tenants will have flown hundreds
of miles each day without a stop.

Two bald eagles at the edge of our woods
are keeping score on poetic justice.
Their nest is filled with tiny twigs, moss
and hollowed bones of trout, moles and kittens.
They know nature's cruelty can be just as stark as ours.
There is a tiger moth that drinks the tears of birds.

Imagine what a bird's shadow signals to someone
locked away from light. Each year, birds traverse
skies filled with obstacles they did not make.
They do not over-think their options. In August,
a ruby-throated hummingbird drank from our feeders.
By December, her wings whirl in Panama.

Love Nest

As spring's heart flutters toward summer,
I have fallen hopelessly for two bald eagles
who sit atop a tall dead pine
scanning our reservoir's dinner menu
for their nesting babes. As the hour darkens,
they calculate the weight of prey.
My schoolgirl crush extends to their nest
fitting just so below the crown
of a tall white pine that marks
the far line of our property.
Their cone-shaped aerie looks delicate
only to visitors stranded on ground.

I am a fool for once unruly branches
woven and knotted like an heirloom
crazy quilt, innards softened by moss,
grass and cornstalks, encircled
by fallen feathers and stray down.
I am in awe of the way the pair
have built this refuge together,
bonding like decorators
over each string, bone and twig.
I am awed by each year's remodeling,
a visual scrapbook of each chick
hatched, fledged, branched and launched.

I adore how each parent warms
the egg, shares the hunt, tears
apart the food, protects the brood,
teaches wind drift, starscapes,
flight patterns. Most of all, I am mad
for their passion—how they return
each season, faithful and filled
with ardor, how they plunge, dive,
swoop, cartwheeling erotica as new
as in their earliest days. As if they
did not know of winter's perils.
As if happy endings always arrived.

A Pre-COVID Bus Ride

City morning light dazzles through
drizzling rain. Passengers are packed
inside like old friends. They smell
of wet wool, musk, floral perfumes.
Their faces shine, luminous in the glow
of tightly gripped cell phones.

Ads promising jobs, training classes,
freedom from addictions and abuses
go unread. Rainbow-hued umbrellas,
crumpled or hooked over railings,
create their own softer rain
moistening briefcases, caps, purses.

We lumber along past busy offices
and coffee spots. Retail gates lift,
street vendors unpack vans, food
trucks open window shelves. Brakes
squeal as passengers pull cords at last
moments, exit, push forward into rain.

Amidst the dissonant din—a woman sits
in a reserved front seat. She cradles two
small bags on her lap. Swift as flight,
she reaches in, out, folds, twists. Colored
paper squares transform to origami birds
of paradise. A sanctuary roosts in our midst.

Bird Sanctuary

When we see the little wooden boat
filled with duck hunters,
we are huddled on the sandy shoreline.
No motor, just the *slap slap* of paddles
on the glistening surface. Each group
is surprised by intrusion. They hope
to set up their blinds, wait for innocents
to leave formation, to be lulled by
mirrored skies and swaying reeds.
We too lack permission to be present.

Sheltered by protected marshes,
there is little to be done but smile,
offer an awkward wave of hand.
Quickened, urgent intakes of breath
follow, the way innocent fall breezes
nuzzle marsh grasses as they drift past.
Once the rowboat floats beyond us,
our collective exhales ripple the waters.

The idea, after all, was to find both
haven and harbor. Even in this cloistered
retreat, we may not be lucky twice.
So, racing against the autumn sun,
we jerk open the humble plastic
bag. My mother's ashes rise, arc
over the waterway, then filter down,
settle, glide away toward Ireland.

The Reincarnation Of Flight

Remembering Louise . . .

Today, as I looked out my window, Louise was there.
Wings spread, feathered claws, golden eyes open,
whiter than the snowy yard, bits of brown and black
thrown in like modest afterthoughts.

I knew her right away. She sat calmly on the ground,
blinking as she scoured for signs of life beneath
frozen layered grasses and February winds
the way she used to search for chords on her guitar.

She watched me gather up my thoughts, waited
for the sound of her name to leave my mouth.
Too soon, she rose high over the meadow, ascending
like Led Zeppelin's solo riff in *Stairway to Heaven*.

I was not eager to wave her on,
but knew her nomadic ways.
Unlike that leap from the subway platform,
this new flight path was filled with grace.

Savoring Winter's Silences

Snow slips, slides, slithers away
from a steel grey sky like soft tears.
All is coated in white as far as anyone
can see. Mounds of downy fluff mix
against stark, darkened tree trunks.
Most are pines savoring their last
stand like a ragtag group of soldiers
who have just heard rumors that
an armistice may arrive soon.
As fat, lacy flakes drift sideways
from treetop to limbs to forest floor,
all is voiceless as a childhood dream.

Hold your breath and you might hear
a faint song as it echoes softly within
the bright, feathery hush of early
morning's translucent light. Perhaps
a snowy owl, a red-crested woodpecker,
a bald eagle. They too respect quiet.
Soon all edges soften. Glacial rock
remnants turn fuzzy, frilly, formless.
Everything is powdered in chalky velvet.
In such serene stillness, we seek forgiveness
as we pretend, for a few sumptuous moments,
that all might bode well for our weary world.

Bird Watcher's Diary*

a staid sport   enjoyed by the few but fervent
fresh air   wooded glens   winding trails
binoculars   strapped like necklaces
spotting scopes ready to deploy
telescopic lenses   tripods
field guides   notepads
pens in jacket pockets
citronella and peppermint

veterans recite tales of hopeful sightings
look   over there   could that be
a cedar waxwing   partly hidden   on that back branch
quiet   isn't that a hooded warbler serenade
just up there   a northern flicker
did you see the long-eared owl   the horned lark
a ruby throat   a grey cheek   a rose breast
an orange crown   a blue wing   just last week

yet somehow   on a sun-dappled afternoon
in the Ramble   birding while Black
proves as challenging   as night driving
or Skittles buying   or cigarette selling
an unleashed dog   an unhinged woman
talking turns to trauma   to terror
once again   cell phones tell the story
this ending better than most   no mourning doves

Murmurations*

My friend and I are talking indignant politics
We are about to cross the Mid-Hudson bridge,
steel sky above, chilly water below,
when a cloud of birds twists, spins above us.

They seek every bare branch, fill them
as if they were summer leaves, then scatter
again like confetti in wind. No one in charge,
yet balance animates all.

Like scat singers, each vibrating note resounds,
rebounds. Each airborne thrum and trill,
purr and prattle sweeps the skies, harmony
clear, like a drummer's brush technique.

Their grace is a loose coordination:
Swing. Smooth. Bebop. Hip Hop. Cool.
Aerial musicians in synchrony, each linked
to the next. We discontented humans drive on.

An Ordinary Day*

> *About suffering they were never wrong* . . .
> —W.H. Auden, "Musee de Beaux Arts"

At first, obituaries sold stories of departures,
of lives we could imagine, might have known.
Each time one began a poem about COVID
losses, daily numbers had mass multiplied.

Most of us feel immune to anonymous
passings. Grave diggers dressed for space travel
make news now as they place a pandemic's
unclaimed dead in Hart Island's trenches.

Louisa Van Slyke, TB victim, was its first
arrival in 1869. Most solitary deaths that filled
these graves are unmarked, numbers punctuating
mossy grasses like dandelion seed heads.

Last respects are paid by Saltmarsh Sparrows
who leave Long Island Sound with morning clouds.
Listen closely—one can faintly hear Bill Withers:
Ain't No Sunshine; Louis Armstrong: *Oh Didn't He Ramble.*

Transformations

Four noisy crows gather
on treetops in Rock Creek Park
to disagree all day long.

One, alone at the far edge dark hickory,
insists, amidst the clattering,
that she is a *Rook, not* a crow.

Her comrades cackle. There is always
someone who thinks she can simply
dare her way to difference.

*It does not matter how much you wish
for mythical possibilities,* they say.
You are a crow, and only murders gain notice.

Rooks demand attention too, she barks.
Think clamor, chess tournaments, parliaments.
Her talons tap like drumsticks against the gnarly bark.

The Rook soars to the tallest tulip poplar,
leaving her girlfriends backlit against golden leaves.
Her song begins at the back of her throat.

Couples Counseling Advice From
Great Horned Owls*

we were busy arguing
when we first heard them
hoo hoo hoooooo hoo hoo
hoo hoo hoooooo hoo hoo
daylight had temporized
we were not eavesdropping
they were adamant
daring us to look outside
even though the wind
had started to whistle its own
mournful freight train song
shaking the leaves
like forgotten laundry
chiding us to catch new sounds

when their forms took shape
at the edge of the woods
hoo hoo hoooooo hoo hoo
hoo hoo hoooooo hoo hoo
we were still squabbling
they were announcing
how shape-shifting works
when you cast your eyes about
to see what you've missed
puff out your throats
rub your bills together
tip up your tails
passion will still matter   if we take notice
if you bring me a mouse

Examining The Heart Of The Matter

In chilled air, leaves drift off,
dive into swirled wind currents.
Tree limbs suddenly revealed,
stark as radiographic slides,
still carry signs of life:
leafy clumps, bits of string,
ribbon, feathers, straw stalks.

These abandoned diaries
of vagabond songbirds
remind me of faded polaroids
once sharp with small details.
Stories of robins, grackles, catbirds,
sparrows sit as exposed
as an emptied apartment complex.

As I study their unveiled remains,
I see how lives take shape around us
even as we barely notice. Now it is
memory of birdsong that remains
on branches as dejected as dispatched
lovers. Empty limbs as epilogue.

Isn't this what we fear most in winter's
icy glare? That nothing will be left
from which to reconstruct those tales
of long journeys south that once felt
so vibrant, so worthy of attention
in a summer afternoon's sympathetic light.

Countercurrents

Our bald eagles are at it again.
Taking turns sitting atop
a sprawling, multi-layered nest
they've been renovating for years.
Each time, new eggs portend
an optimism we humans often lack.
We hear them squawking at hawks
who circle too close—bold, belligerent
on this grey February morning.
Branches snap, crackle in shear
of wind. Ice skims the reservoir
like wisps of an old man's beard.

A raft of ducks float along the water,
feathers ruffled by chilled air.
I try to imagine how their blood flows
from webbed feet to heart and back,
how they avoid freezing as we hug
ourselves to stay warm while we watch
them rotate between clumps of white
like slow-moving carnival bumper cars.
Fish gills use those same backward
currents to transfer oxygen from water
into their blood. Another marvel
of nature's inventiveness.

It is at moments like this one that
ecological calamity feels less certain.
A steady rhythm hums, thrums along
like an orchestra as it tunes up before
a symphony begins. Pulled along
by such placid days, the timbre
of time reverts back toward memory's
glaze. We are lulled into acceptance

of circumstances we have grown
used to as well as those we may never
fully comprehend. It leaves us caught,
unprepared, for whirlpools to come.

How To Write A Woodpecker Poem

In writing your poem, tell the truth as you know it.
Tell your truth. Remember that poetry is life distilled...
                                        —Gwendolyn Brooks

I.

I thought Jack DeJohnette had set
up his drum set in my back yard.
A woodpecker the size of a mallard
hammered its beak into an old apple tree.
Its head was red as a ripe Heirloom
tomato. Black and white feathers shone
like sequins against a lava crest
as the bird curved in and out, used its
ivory beak to carve through mottled
bark in search of sap, nuts, beetles.
With each *rat tat, rat tat, rat tat* call,
each *knock, knock, knock, knock, knock*
reply, a tree transformed to sound stage.
The more I watched, the more it seemed
as if a Diva drummer had settled in
for a long gig—Nikki Glaspie, Bobbye Hall,
Terri Lynne Carrington. Like a starstruck fan
at a stage door, I ventured closer in hopes of eye
contact, maybe even a selfie. True to her star
stature, she granted me a measure of time
before lifting away from echoes of her performance.
As she sailed off into the pine forest,
I sensed kinship more than spectacle.
Each day I wait for one more crimson splash,
for those percussive beats of our rhyming hearts.

II.

Editorial feedback sucks sometimes.
My editor critiques my ode to a giant
woodpecker that briefly transformed
my Woodstock yard into a drumbeat-rich
concert venue one sparkling summer day.
Her redlined marginal notes say
I am waiting for the poem to be more,
to move beyond describing that woodpecker.
But, I thought, wasn't that the point?
A morning had begun like any other —
coffee in hand, bad news emblazoned
boldfaced in the not-so-fine print.
I nursed aches, grievances, ticked off lists
of chores, demands, regrets. I sighed
at how time raced by, even when I felt
encased in amber. And then, in one sudden,
swirling blaze of red, black, white,
a day turned into a miracle.

III.

I am long, tall, talented. Dressed
in my best onyx and pearl finery.
My head's as red as Judy Garland's Oz shoes,
which one might think I'm wearing
as I tap dance on this apple tree.
You could have heard me miles away
if you took time to look past deafening
daily news drumbeats. I beckon you
outside, to join me as I move, sway,
gyrate like Elvis from branch to branch.
If you follow my lead, you will hear
music everywhere. We will pirouette
across this leafy stage awaiting applause.
Today, you will believe in reincarnation.

What Do Old Birds Talk About?

Once upon a time, aches, pains
were not my constant consorts.
I walked about with no falling fears;
raced for buses, paced by little
more than a random schedule; sped
across a tennis court, racquet
readied to slam the ball across
the net; hiked over roots, brambles,
aiming for thinned air panoramas.

Wasn't that just yesterday? Who
can calculate the warp speed of
decline? Today, I watch our nesting
pair of eagles as they circle skies
like ancient calligraphers. How do
they manage time's rough passages,
its humorless ravages? Do complaints
and grievance fill up their air space
when wings molt and talons weaken?

Perhaps they reminisce, share anecdotes
of bygone exploits as they congregate
at reservoir's edge. Or remonstrate
against ill fates as they traverse tree
lines of fading pines. I'd like to think
that they luxuriate in psychedelic
highs of limitless skies or flashbacks
of brazen breezes and unfettered flights.

Anthropomorphizing

We found a lawn spinner
that resembles a loon.
Hammered it into ground
near a tree-shaded patio.
It flaps its wings
like a wild creature stuck
standing in our woods
stranded yet hopeful.
Black, white, a large red eye.
Its wings flash, flutter, whirl.
It winds, turns, revolves.
How easily trapping
occurs. How difficult
parting. Yesterday,
a whirr of wings—tan, grey
—a horned owl or
an eager eaglet—flew
down maybe to see up close
if rescue was possible.
Or else just to give thanks
for the joy of flight.

Confessions Of A Casual Bird Watcher

This late October morning, I ventured out for a walk
along our creek where rose pink golden leaves saw
their future selves twisting and bobbing, pierced in halves
and quarters like scattered coins. The day began raw,

the way late fall can evoke a tear, like dew
or a lamentation. I passed through fronds of grass
once home to purple martins feasting on a wall
of milkweed. I moved aside to let our old tortoise pass

(he's lived here longer than I) and sensed his eyes
were also clouded by sadness. Above, geese headed abroad
following ancestral cartography. I wondered if they thought
about how earth transforms each year or just flew ahead,

unquestioning, into thinning layers of blue. No one is cautious
enough these days, especially birds. Habitats thin, each crumb
powders, drifts off —dispersed like a billion feathers
silenced. Songbirds of every octave were once at home here.

Now, they are faint memories bleached bone white as ocean reefs.
Sequoias, Rubberwoods, Kapoks have formed a jagged seam
across the planet, no longer able to offer shade from a hot noon
sun. I want to join the leaves in my creek for a swim.

Mourning Dove Portfolios

Outside my window, four doves converse
on spider webs of oak and maple branches.
Fattened by bird seed, they peer out
over the long-wintered meadow
like savvy scouts searching the scenery
for signs of trouble ahead.

I want to call out that *trouble,* indeed,
has arrived. The work of doves has never
been so essential. As they shake
out their grey feathers against these
sharp winds, I am betting on savvy
instinct. Our Capitol is under siege.

Some days I can hear their whistle—
a high-pitched whine from their wings
designed to scare off predators. Their
pigeon relatives flew messages for kings
and armadas, Caesar and Genghis Kahn.
Imagine the noise they must have made.

Most doves have ten thousand feathers.
In a dream I watched as flocks circled the mall,
wings whinnying beneath a pale sun.
In the beating, bleating air, fluff, tufts,
plumage sifted down, cushioned the ground.
Soon silence was everywhere. Soft as snow.

Flightless Birds

My grandmother's ink drawing
of a Dodo bird was steeped
in detail, as if she had tended
to its nest herself, watched as it
hatched, thrived. She perused
each wing tip, parsed each shade,
each shadowed plume, each plane
of beak, each scaled dark talon.

In her rendering, the bird
shared a wry smile, as if
the joke was on all of us.
I imagined how it must have
soared across its island home
but she told me that the Dodo
was *flightless,* bound to earth
the way we humans were.

She said its relatives
were pigeons. I peered closely
at its pear-shaped body, its smooth
head, hooked, green-tinged beak,
its fat yellow legs and curly rear
wisps of tail feathers. It was
hard to fathom its failure
to lift away from land.

She told me the bird no longer
lived, done in by carelessness,
perhaps more than deliberate
cruelty. Exposed to natural
perils as sailors arrived at its
Mauritius island home to fell
trees, clear-cut thick jungles.
Extinct, like Pterodactyls.

Back then, I searched for
a moral to sum up the Dodo's
tale: to fly was key to survival.
Later on, as I learned how humans
are the likely cause of almost
every lost, beautiful thing, I knew
that being flightless was the least
of it. Wings are the last resort of angels.

Journal Entry: Great Horned Owl

Some say a poem is never
just about its subject matter.
Metaphor matters as much as
lyrical style or creative rhyme.

I thought of that today as I peered
from my perch at the forest's edge.
My grey striped feathers, tinged with white,
ruffled in the sharp autumn breeze.

A fat squirrel hurried to hide
beside a slab of once-glacial
granite that now punctuates clusters
of echinacea, lavender, sedum.

Normally I hunt as night drifts
over the meadow, slips onto
tree limbs like grey stockings.
But today, sunlight caught my gaze.

I could see into the windows
of the blue house where two women
have made their own roost. One of them
brings seeds and nuts out all winter.

Some nights my audiobiography
wakes her. Today, just as I landed on
a thick branch, intent on my hunt,
she caught my eye and smiled.

We paused, like a brief inhale.
But then, open sky promised other
viewpoints. Sometimes, we glimpse
as much as we need to know.

Winter Navigation Lessons

our driveway looks
like mirrored glass
you would see yourself
quite clearly as you
tumbled downward
right before bones
snapped splintered
all beneath a golden sun
is it better to remain
indoors as the radio
bleats news of democracy
crumpled
last year's inaugural
optimism
now a highway pileup
pandemic stats climbing
despite masks and boosters
if we ventured out
past treacherous ice
we would hear
northern cardinals whistle
they have worries too
but for now
they stay aloft
bursts of crimson
dancing with wind

Mourning Our Dead

A brown and white speckled egg
about the size of a thumbnail lies
broken on a grey wooden deck.
The pale yellow embryo landed
at an angle, its tiny feet tinged
with orange. Its nervous mother
had been squawking at passersby
from a nest perched on a drainpipe.

It's not just coronaviruses that play
havoc with expectations. Morning air
is warmed by sunshine. A day begins
with sunrise over pines and creek
water reflecting its rays as if votive
candles were tossed from its banks.
A meadowlark's *weet weet* mixes with a
sparrow's *see see,* reverent as a Shacharit prayer.

In The Wind. I*

Once upon a time, I could spend a lazy day pulling
beetles from inside dead pines and cedars. I tapped
on their trunks to stir things up. No one likes loud noise.
Once they moved, my beveled beak grooved on soft

wood, gashed it open, peeled away layers of bark,
sucked up a sumptuous meal. I could polish off grubs,
eggs, seeds and acorns, all while morning's haze still
hovered over the forest floor like a muslin shroud.

I preferred swamplands, marshes. People always
said I was the flashy type, with my flame-red crest
and bristling black and white feathers. I enjoyed
perching in treetops behind curtains of cypress,

like an opera star awaiting the music's swell before
she takes center stage. Now, loggers drag off my larvae-
filled feasts, ponds clog with shredded plastic bags,
my roost holes have been displaced by factory smoke.

Back in the day, Audubon painted me—a rather good
likeness, truth be told. Songs were written. Rewards
were offered. Photographs were shared like religious icons.
Hunters waited in the wings.

It is better to be boring. Unknown, unlisted, unwatched.
So, if some day you spy a splash of crimson amidst tall conifers,
say a prayer, then walk away. Think of me now as *in the wind,*
a fugitive from all that can and does go wrong.

Quantum Entanglements

Each autumn, bar-tailed godwits
flap, flap, flap, flap their wings
for days on end. From southern Alaska
to New Zealand. Seven thousand miles.
Some soar three or four miles above ground.
They do not stop for food, water, respite.
Like marathon runners, they bulk up
before flight, double their weight,
use fat for fuel, stay tuned into the zone.
They shape-shift to follow magnetic lines.

When godwits finally land in Christchurch,
bells peal in welcome. In March, their chosen
route of return passes through tidal flats
in China's Yellow Sea. No one knows how
they stay aloft. Survival demands they move
as one. Their spellbinding stories travel
the globe like Einstein's theory of relativity.
When light bends, everyone follows its flame.
Perhaps this is optimism defined.
Sing to me. Our harmony will permeate skies.

How To Tally Some Of Our Abundant Losses*

I scan bird lists at random times   when skies grow still
take out a sharpie   cross off each third name
do it again   for every letter
for every listing   three billion gone
across species   habitats   territories
ecosystems   a fractional span of time
in history's sweep   yet we know about absences
absences are heavy   we are weighed down by silence

silences
where skies at dawn   once throbbed
with warbler chorales   with dusky murders of crows

where a cast of hawks circled   plagues of grackles
or dove cotes   where geese flocks aimed south

alongside a siege of herons,   where starling murmurations

thickened   a sky like a black stew
we would like to have flown
with them   across earth's curvatures

we would like to have known them   before they slipped past us
quiet as whispers

nothing rises above us
our losses grow   feathered with sorrows

try it yourself   start anywhere   cross out each third name

Cabot's tragopans   Chestnut bellied partridges
Cackling geese   Chilean flamingos
Cactus wrens   Chilean hawks
California quail   Chimney swifts
Campbell albatross   Chinstrap penguins

Canada geese
Canaries
Canvasbacks
Cape beron geese
Cape grassbirds
Cape sparrows
Cardinals
Carrier pigeons
Cassowaries
Cattle tyrants
Cedar waxwings
Chats
Chickadees
Chinese egrets

Chubut steamer ducks
Chuck will's widows
Cockatiels
Cockatoos
Condors
Cormorants
Cowbirds
Crab-plovers
Cranes
Crescent chest puffers
Crows
Cotingas
Cuckoos
Curassows

La Clairvoyance*

after La Clairvoyance *by René Magritte*

My house is filled with birds. They dangle from ceilings,
rest on windowsills, decorate bookshelves, look out
at their livelier cousins who land in the lilac bush,
make their nests in tangles of wisteria or tops of drainpipes.
One friend, an acclaimed non-bird lover, says she
must breathe deeply before she walks inside. As if
she fears they might all rise up against her,
a Hitchcockian murmuration, closing off escape routes.
Once I stood under the nine-foot wingspans
of California condors, realizing I might be prey.

My love affair with birds is deep. First, the dove,
an optimistic icon from childhood Sunday school lessons.
Other miracles: Cardinals—flash of flame against a hedge.
Humble robins, brazen blue jays. Park pigeons crowding
a bench for thrown lunch scraps. A nesting pair of eagles
who remain at our woods' edge through ice and storms.
Red-capped woodpeckers. Great horned owls. Herons
who soar like ballet dancers above the creek.
Even wild turkeys, ignoring laughter as they work their way
across the meadow, pretending to be peacocks.

Perhaps birds offer insight into ways we humans
might evolve, improve. How we might rise
above petty complaints that bind us like yardbirds.
Each year, they traverse earth's arc, maneuver
past wind turbines, smog, seacoasts, cypress swamps,
skyscraper windows, scraps of plastic netted in treetops,
yet return to lay their eggs in the heart of an aging oak.
We look at an egg, yet imagine a future of flight.

Creating The Sounds of Music*

I.

In autumn, not every bird is prone to sing.
To conserve energy, their brains begin shrinking.
Body mass reduces. An altered state
of lighter need takes hold. Desire to migrate
moves them from tree to air. Magnetic fields
guide them. As they soar, wind drift shields
their aerial patterns, turns them fluid as a paintbrush.
Their flights are long. They must avoid ambush
by poisoned waters, airplane wings, boys who shoot
rocks, plastics, windowpanes. Each known route
is possessed with evolving dangers that could
end songs waiting to return to elm, oak, dogwood.

II.

When I was young, most of all I loved to sing.
Only much later, I discovered how nothing
is guaranteed by desire. My voice, lightweight
at best, proved better suited to be an adequate
chorus member. With luck, one learns to push
aside wishful thinking. This is where a wood thrush
comes in. We learn the value of staying mute
when avian ribbons of harmony salute
each season, surprising all who briefly stood
still to listen. What if each day we could
all embrace this practice—let music cover us
like raindrops, soaking every pore with solace.

III.

Instead of shouting, we humans should try to sing.
Reaching for high C instead of weapons might bring
us closer to songbirds whose throat muscles vibrate
against a raindrop-sized organ. They calibrate
each hum, thrum, each murmured melody
like a fine orchestral overture, an elegy
to meadows, backyard brush piles, lilac bush,
to all the humble sights we miss, as we rush
toward predictable corners of dispute,
discord, our moral certainty absolute.
Even if every note is far from perfect,
birdsong can still become hope's architect.

Who Can Hear A Love Song?*

The Kauai O'o stopped singing
decades ago. Its lilting, bell-like
sounds drifted like silken strands
through jungle forests, lifted air
in humid wetlands, shifted rainbowed
skies. One hopeful mating call can
still be heard on tape. The last male
chirps, whistles, sighs for thrill of
romance. The female, dead five years
now, will not reply. Still, his voice rises
through mist and rain. Bright yellow
feathers shuffle against dark brown
plumage as he shifts long legs to better
amplify his song through tangled vines.
As he tries to court her with twinkling
trills of music, does he ever question
why silence is her sole retort? Or does
he, like poets everywhere, design words,
stir, spill, spin them aloft, in prayer
that a passionate audience will appear?

Sounds of music when birds have left us

Three billion birds have disappeared
like proteins gone missing
in a brain. Bachman's warbler,
preserved in hazy photographs.

Or Mozart's starling, said to have
inspired his Seventh Piano
Concerto. And ascending larks,
as inscribed by Ralph Vaughn Williams.

The cetti's warbler
whose trill inspired first notes
of Beethoven's Second, its last
movement filled with dainty chirping.

In Respighi's *Pines of Rome,* a
nightingale dazzles. Now there are fewer
song sparrows, blackbirds, doves,
whooping swans and finches

to echo wind serenades.
Where will music go
when skies have emptied,
when memory no longer holds birdsong?

Part III:

Flight. Reimagined

*Unclose your mind. You are not a prisoner.
You are a bird in flight, searching the skies for dreams.*
—Haruki Murakami

*I hope you love birds too. It is economical.
It saves going to heaven.*
—Emily Dickinson

Man Talking To Bird*

after a painting of the same title by Bill Traylor

Bill Traylor has captured
a conversation about
how to survive our lives.

Two creatures leaning in,
staring at each other
as if little time is left.

Each perched atop a listing chimney
on adjacent, asymmetrical boxes
blue and white with orange doors.

The man holds a long, thin stick in one hand,
reaches out with the other. The bird's beak is sharp.
Its tailfeathers are long. They list toward each other.

They are dwarfed by a world
off-kilter. With closed doorways.
Unless they pay attention, both will fall.

No one else can hear
or judge them. Black bird, red
man. Tan sky. Blue boxes.

What if it were simple
like this? Reach out.
Listen.
Soar.

The Future Of Civilization*

There are twenty polar bears.
Their ivory coats cast a luminescent
glow against gunmetal grey skies,
seaweed-toned mists and volcanic
rock formations with a mica sheen.
Some bears peer out from behind
the weather station's glassless windows,
as if they are about to welcome
guests for late afternoon tea.

Others wander past rusted canisters,
dismantled iron pipes which lie in heaps
like broken children's toys. Skeletons
of windmill towers dot the landscape.
The drone camera hovers overhead.
It has been specially designed
to photograph quietly, like some
Cold War spy, huddled behind
an indistinct black Nash Rambler.

The aging fortress, abandoned
thirty years ago by Russian scientists,
seems well suited to its new denizens.
Its structures have stayed mostly upright,
wooded roof slats still in place, copper
chimney pipes aimed at the heavens.
Flashes of ochre, lemon yellow
and pale blue paint blend on exterior
walls, like chiaroscuro woodcuts.

The bears are relaxed, curious as cats.
A few stroll about on neon green
mossy ground. One imagines
how they might sink down into
its spongey surface, each footstep
leaving behind a webbed pawprint
large as a cast iron frying pan.

When sunshine licks away thick fog,
the bears posture themselves like
Mediterranean sunbathers. One can
almost see them smile as they loll
on the hillside, watching the Arctic Ocean
transform to ribbons of lapis lazuli
as sunshine emerges like an eager child.
Careful eyes keep tabs on swimming seals.

The photographs remind me
of the ubiquitous sheep that dot
Ireland's hillsides bordered by shades
of green, ancient stone mounds, an
endless sea. Lately, our thoughts of
polar bears tend to be Shakespearean:
a cruel hunger slimming them down
to bone, eyes gazing without seeing,
as they drift on melting floes of ice.

But these bears have merrier tales to tell.
On this island refuge, danger has receded.
Human calamities have no place here
where Wooly Mammoths once roamed.
Our alabaster mammals swim, dive, romp
and range free as ivory gulls. Staring at
the drone, they seem to be saying to us: *Move
out. Move on. We are doing great without you.*

If I Were A Monarch Butterfly

I'd play Django Reinhardt's
gypsy jazz as I rambled.
Like Romani everywhere,
my roots are temporary,
my wings all bling, swing,
my story backed with chords,
percussion, sweep of strings.
Improvisation keeps me
aloft as I glide through air
like flecks of sunlight adrift
on morning tides. Fueled
by lilt of violins, acoustic
guitar arpeggios, wind
shear keeps me dancing
from milkweed to magenta
cone flower to golden
jungle marigolds. Tune in
to my background story,
a glissando shift from bass
to highest C notes. I can't be
constrained, reined in, pinned down.
Watch me soar from hot club
to blues bar, from waltz to swing
dance. Follow me as I cross
mountains, boundaries, border walls,
from *Clouds* to that elusive
Mansion of Our Dreams.

To Be Blessed

To be blessed, I always thought,
was like being able to walk on water.
A miracle of positive thinking.

Everyone around you sinks,
arms and legs thrashing like cymbals,
while you still hear the sun's orchestral chords.

To be *blessed,* on the other hand,
was what the sales clerk said about the day she urged you to have
after she wrapped your holiday gifts and tied their bows.

To be blessed was to have your best friend of 45 years
remember your name again as you walk with her
through once lovingly planted lush gardens.

I can still see her lavender and lupine,
laurel and lobelia. I shade my eyes against
the shine of orange Koi darting past lotus blossoms.

To be blessed is to see two eagles nesting in a treetop
as I drive home from running errands,
amidst radio chatter about terrifying times to come.

To be blessed is to listen to Miles Davis:
Kind of Blue and *Sketches of Spain*
as calm and cool as neon moss against my cheek

To be blessed is knowing that even the fierce rage
that fills my body like fire climbing walls
might be tamped down if I took a walk in my woods

past our stream and its little waterfall.
As my boots kick leaves away, I head for the pond
where walking on water seems possible. Even flying.

Flight. Reimagined. I

You have left me. Your whispered promises lie scattered
like starlings. Red-breasted robin songs turn discordant,
as if the bird has gone off-key, blown astray by wind turbines.
The morning after we are over (Over!), I wake early,
as if I can still reach back into yesterday's reality,
caress it as I once did your incandescent body.
But, even left here alone with thoughts swirling,
my memories still aglow like watermelon's red thunder,
I am not as sad as I might have predicted at the start,
or even as recently as Friday. What do any of us
really know of regret? We deposit our grief
at gravesites, hospital corridors, hospice chapels.

Love does not always end with a final parting,
just as it does not end at the banks of the river Styx.
Even as the ferry makes off with the body, one can find
comfort in absence. The way that dead fireflies still glow.
Do not shroud me with sorrow. Today I am at the beginning
of the rest of my life. Once you said - so softly I almost missed it—
that I was like a narcotic to you. At the time, that thought
seemed thrilling, like an ever-elusive addict-chasing high.
But now I know I do not want to feel anesthetized by love.
I want to cradle the thought of it in my hand
like a tiny fledgling. Tell it there is always hope,
light, blue sky. That flight can be a thing of exultation.

In The Beginning Was The Fear

outside my window   no one is lost for words
cardinals speak in two-part whistles
cherie cherie   chip chip chip   cherie cherie
quick bursts of sound   then softer trills
no demands   nothing silences them
every day a channel to open skies

we should remember this
when timidity overwhelms our spirits
maybe it is as simple as conquering fears
that have strangled us   tangled our faith
jangled our nerves   does anyone even know us
or care to make that leap

what makes us care
what anyone ever thinks of us
once I walked into a room filled with strangers
ended up falling in love
the less we expect the more we discern
today I am a tangerine bird singing to wind

Re-Thinking Basic Dance Steps

Lately, I have been thinking a lot
about dancing—how I always imagined
it should feel. Gravity left behind,
shaking its weary head,
as I spin, turn, shimmy, spiral
past memory's drumbeat. As if
one could *tap tap tap* far away
from troubled turmoil to discover a brand
new stage where lengthening shadows
of regret are the only things
waiting in the wings. Today, I stared
at photographs from Kabul's airport.

It is hard to fathom such despair that sends
one racing on foot down an airplane runway,
clinging to jumbo jet wings as if they were dance
partners. As they strained for the upward lift,
the earth-bound crowd stranded below
understood how fickle prom dates could be,
how we must become our own choreographers
to arrive at the airport gates, to be invited
on board. With each trip, slip, stumble, tumble,
one sees how certainty of death can also mean
escape, albeit with less rhythm, less fanfare
than was craved in yesterday's richer light.

what is a dream after all

what is a dream after all
maybe it's a bird
soaring south over checkered corn
lime green grasses silken wheat
riding wind columns
like a hobo on the rails

or is a dream a voice
that coaxes us toward safety
or escape   or a long walk
through a desert
clutching a rosary
and a half-empty bottle of stale water

maybe a dream can walk
out of a convenience store
light up a new cigarette
joke with friends
drive home listening to
Ain't Nobody's Business

maybe a dream   is louder than we think
maybe it could wake up a crowd
imagine how a dream might swim across a river
and emerge clean and rested and whole
on the other side   safe in a parent's arms
ready for a new life

Cease Fire*

We are not always happy at the news.
Though one might think we would rejoice.
There is always that uptick in dying
before the eerie silence settles in
like dust filtered on late day's twilight.
Peace tiptoes on death's long shadows.
Of course the ones who agree are never
those who gather up body parts like leaves.

These are the questions no one asked us:
Are we tired of our eardrums breaking apart?
How long must our children sit, dazed and
bleeding, for photographic portraiture?
How will we turn growing piles of bricks and
rubble back to something called a neighborhood?
Did we cry as we left our once green gardens
in search of rubber rafts on open seas?

If there are good answers to these questions,
perhaps peacekeepers are jotting them down
in their computers or cease fire notebooks.
Here is my question for them: Will one of you
be here to walk out with me to the marketplace
just before it starts? In that often forgotten
moment when we place our lives at risk
for a taste of cardamom-spiced coffee.

The Languages We Need To Hear

sometimes we are surrounded
by silences as loud as orchestras
as we lean in to listen
a clock tick lengthens
a pinprick reverberates
a bronze gong echoes
circles of constant motion
as leaves rustle   shuffle
as wind whooshes   swishes
whoops like wild laughter
atop tall conifers

not every sound
is in a language we recognize
some languages are not
even sounds at all
they are colors
a blood orange harvest moon
an aquamarine iceberg
champagne stars
evanescent in a midnight darkened sky
drops of moisture pale as cornsilk
blink from leaf   or cheek

a pair of eagles call out
using their own vocabularies
as they circle over a russet meadow
filled with monarch wings
purring like cats
some words are gesture
cupped in our hands like
phosphorescent fireflies
fingers touch   open wide
luminous for one instant

sometimes a moment
of silence can be heard
by someone
because it is
a prayer

How I Learned To Fly Like A Cat

Not so long ago, each day's events
were fluid—birdwatching melded to
gardening to writing to making soup.
Now, I am bound to laboratory
schedules and injection regimens.
My veins are being filled with pale liquids
with unpronounceable names.
It is still too early to know tales of other patients.
Perhaps one never does. Most stare
at cell phones or the beige linoleum floor.

Cindy, the IV nurse, is cheerful. She goes
about her business of wiping, flushing,
hooking up, disconnecting without comment.
She has seen it all and keeps her opinions
close. On the day insurrectionists spilled into
the Capitol, she declined to turn the television
away from HGTV. Maybe that *was* an opinion.
I won't ask. I want everything to go smoothly,
without kinks or fuss. And so I admire
her sun-dappled pots of philodendron.

Some days I feel like an astronaut readying
for a spacewalk. Survival depends on cables
that link back to the mothership, wires threaded
just so, receptors charged up, reporting each data
point so it can be read before a red alert lights up
the monitors. Other days I pretend I am
Félicette, the French tuxedo cat, implanted with
electrodes for her sixties space ride. I'm still within
my nine lives, depending how one counts.
Bound by this filament to distant galaxies, I'll nap.

Is There A Cure For Sadness?

When the moon stops by your bed at night,
ask her if she knows a cure for sadness.
Tell her how you've longed for hope to ignite

instead of that constant grieving poets write
about when eyeing doorways tinged with madness.
When the moon bends near your bed at night,

remember that not everything bathed in light
is destined to impart wisdom or gladness.
Tell her how you long for hope to ignite

like falling stars that tease us from great height
before they disappear into abstractness.
When the moon climbs into your bed at night,

don't be afraid to demand more than sleight
of hand. Tell her you desire much more than this.
Tell her how you've hungered for hope to ignite

each tiny pore, each tingling nerve. Despite
everything you fear in midnight's eerie vastness,
if the moon does join you in your bed tonight,
remind her how long you've waited for hope to ignite.

Observing The Passage Of Venus

Every eight Aprils,
we can admire Venus
as she brushes just past
Alcyone, a Pleiades
Sister, blowing
kisses. A gibbous moon
will dazzle us with light
as these hook ups are framed
on walls of dusky skies.
We are close to perigee.

In morning's glaze, lunar
pleasures shift to Saturn,
Jupiter, Mars. Watch them line
up like girlfriends, as they
arrive home from a late
night dance party high on
stardust, still dressed
in festive finery. As spring's twilight
passes to dawn, we give
thanks for these renderings.

Our planetary artists
proffer lush canvases
when we are most in need,
transform our point of view
away from dark places.
When museums shuttered,
these incandescent murals
layered with star clusters
allowed us a new chance
to ponder infinity.

Ode To Companionship

Microbes hide in clouds near
Venus. We do not know
anything more, yet joy
of company dazzles.

Once some able swimmer
might have sliced through azure
waters like a seal, then
dried off beneath a moon.

Her tiny boat ferried
her toward an island
filled with mica that glittered
like a volcanic halo.

Maybe she held a curved
pale peach shell in her palm,
placed it against her ear,
heard an ocean's echo.

Hope In The Unseen

The Perseverance Rover carries a plaque
honoring health-care workers who have
battled COVID-19. Even or because
no one is there to read it, the gesture seems
right. The Red Planet has always
teased and tempted. What better
way to escape our troubles than to ride
along with science toys tumbling down
toward ancient riverbeds? Join the search
beneath crusted ridges for lessons
from once-lonely beings who also
harbored thoughts of deliverance.

Exploring The Limits Of Curiosity

Sometimes, this pandemic makes us feel aloft,
alienated from our known worlds.
Aspiring to be engaged, we clamber about,
looking deep into memory holes, digging through
detritus we barely recall. As we gather, search,
sift and sort, we shake our heads in wonder.

What once was life now lies dust-bound,
huddled in closet corners, buried in back yards,
curled beneath the bed. We peer in at a diorama,
spectrometers at the ready. Every molecule has a story
waiting to be extracted with the precision of a diamond
cutter. We want to be cosmic archeologists.

There is barely a mirrored glimmer left, amid rock slab
sediment and swirling dust, of what once might have
been true. As each day rambles into the next, our search
continues unabated. Look at this faint imprint
that might once have been a smile, this hint
of moisture that might once have been a tear.

In The Wind. II

In Fall's brazen winds, I wonder what I might find
flirting amidst speckled leaves: acorn husks, twine bits,
seed pods from our Hickory that land unaligned
by rhythm or design on our driveway—a blitz
of weaponry that sabotages without warning.
Some days, nature's debris is too heavy for breezes
to carry it away. The rainstorm stopped this morning
but gusts linger like a scorned lover. It pleases
me to stand outside, hair rustling, taking flight
briefly like some sparrow might before winging around,
returning to safety. I want my sorrows light
so currents will disperse them far from ground
that roots me here. When I search skies for some trace
of you, I beg this wind to be gentle as your embrace.

When Hope Is The Thing We Want To Convey*

a Golden Shovel after "Hope Is The Thing
With Feathers" by Emily Dickinson

It is quite a challenge to write a poem about hope.
Not too trite, not too cloying or sad. Love lost is,
inevitably, a tale of optimism once held close—the
broken heart unknown at the outset before something
shattered like tired bones, before we imagined life with-
out a lover who once transformed our heart to feathers
fluttering wildly when they called out our name. That
ode to a future filled with ardent touch perches,
dusty and stained, on a sagging wooden bookshelf in
the attic of my mind. I cannot bring myself to tell the
stories using new perspectives into a troubled soul
shorn of its light source. Think of imprecations and
prayers rising from darkened prison cells. Who sings
the final chorus of a hymnal's psalms or shouts the
robust *Amens*—often it is hope's messenger whose tune
soars into the cosmos like a volcanic plume, without
a backward look. Yet capturing that feeling is the
real magic. Anyone can assemble some random words
on paper but how does one know they will succeed? And
will anyone be moved to greater insight? One never
knows at a poem's beginning whether a line stops
a listener mid-stride, causing her to reminisce, marvel at
the way an idea suddenly alights, makes sense of it all.

A Brief History Of Optimism

I wanted to study optimism's burnished history
to see if it might lighten my life.
Perhaps its arc bends like Einstein's theory.

In the eighteenth century,
optimisme was thought to mean
the best of all possible worlds.

Voltaire made fun of it
in *Candide*—Dr. Pangloss
never had a darkened moment.

It is harder today to avoid darkness.
It fills every news vehicle, spills
overboard, gallons of ink at a time.

Galileo measured Earth's revolutions
around the sun. Guilty of heresy, he still marked
each movement from his cell window.

Harriet Tubman bent over double, crawled
at night through fields, forests, swamplands.
She knew a sun could rise on freedom.

Nelson Mandela spent twenty-seven years
relocating rocks at Robben Island. He believed
in apartheid's incandescent end.

On Earth Day, Wynn Bruce traveled from Colorado
to set himself on fire. As he burned, he made
no sound, hoping he would be heard.

As shells first fell from dulled skies, Asya Serpinska
stayed in Ukraine to care for dogs, cats, a lion.
This is how we are human, she said.

In Karkhiv, municipal workers braved dark,
din of death to plant daffodils along deserted roadways.
They sparkled like coins in a fountain.

Sandy Hook ten years past, our President speaks
once more about grief and loss. Each daybreak,
parents still wave to children boarding school buses.

Birds may be the greatest optimists of all.
Arctic terns migrate from Pole to Pole. No other
species ever sees as much sunlight.

Optimists call to us like nightingales.
There is no other choice. There is no other sound.
To live in this world we must be willing to listen.

What It Might Mean To Catch A Passing Asteroid

Recently, a school bus-sized
asteroid sped past South America.
A close encounter, warned NASA
engineers. Last fall, they knocked one
off its earth-bound course the way
we might kick a soccer ball or wield
a croquet mallet to avoid defeat.
We are always hoping to alter
trajectories, to avoid the loss
of everything we counted on before
anyone knew better. Remember
when we were young, believing in a
world within our control? Before
we began losing people as easily
as scattered coins or stones that fall
from trouser pockets. Before we
understood that second chances
are rare as osmium crystals.

This latest asteroid shifted course,
moved toward a new orbit. Our skies
are brimming with space rocks heading
toward deserts or cities (no one knows
which or when). Some days it feels as if
we are all dinosaurs at extinction's edge.
In the meanwhile, some people cannot
even drive down a street without
calamity, as blows rain down
from all directions. Compassion
feels as distant as floating space rocks.
Maybe next time we should hitch a ride,
soar past our earth-bound planet plagued
by traumas and troubles. As we rotate

toward the cosmos in geosynchronous
orbits, we might gaze at passing
stars, planets, galaxies, see how
red blinking lights could still be beautiful.

Cloud Cover*

At first, there was just a Lilliputian
cloud. It was so negligible one might
have missed it altogether. Like a cataract.
But it grew bigger, began to darken.
Before long, it had multiplied into
several cloud patches. Each shifted
to a different corner of the sky,
staked out a position. Refused to
move. Dared other clouds to approach
at their peril. The once-azure sky
vanished. Instead, shadows loomed
overhead like prehistoric birds of prey.

At first, few people worried. They knew
shadows need some light to survive.
But the shade expanded. Umbras were
everywhere. They asked *What can we do?*
Thoughts were exchanged. Statistics recorded.
Silhouettes were measured. Dialogue
faltered, flailed, failed. Prayers met silence.
Candles were lit. Flashlight sales grew.
Batteries grew scarce. Campfires flickered
throughout day and night. Their smoke made
it harder to breathe or see. Night vision goggles
were issued to all eligible households.

Soon, the sky was so thickened that memories
numbed, vanished. Books picturing seabirds,
flowers, forests sold out. Libraries kept
waiting lists of tales about people whose lives
were bathed in sunshine. The populace struggled
to recall days at ocean's edge, feet splayed
in wheat-colored sand, a beloved's hand
dappled with light. Shoulders sunburned

from neighborhood meetings and protest marches
soon paled to ghostly reveries. Last to fade
were visions of school playgrounds filled with
children, sneakers aglow with sparkling lights.

Villanelle For Black Holes*

Everything once loved disappears into its massive vortex.
A space so vast, so far removed, we turn to science
to help us fathom its impact, repair its deadly effects.

Numbers alone pose a challenge to our cerebral cortex.
We desire peaceful stories, not tales of violence,
not seeing everything once loved disappear into a massive vortex.

Mathematics can be a useful science, even when we are perplexed
by facts that break us, leave us praying or stunned to silence.
Who can help us fathom impacts, repair deadly effects?

A friend, shot by her husband as she descended her steps
to go to work, left her baby to grow with others' guidance.
Everyone once loved can be disappeared into its massive vortex.

So many things look lovely from afar. Toy-like objects
tease us with their likely power but their devastation defiles us
as we try to fathom their impact, repair their deadly effects.

Colorized, black holes turn orange-red-gold, with flecks
of white light that flicker at their edges. These images beguile us.
Yet everything once loved still disappears into a massive vortex
as we try to fathom its impact, repair its deadly effects.

Infinity's Memoirs: As Told
By The James Webb Telescope

One Christmas morning, as a scarlet sun
gave birth to a crimson sea,
a metal canister arced into the sky.
On board, mirrors as tightly
folded as origami birds,
will gather memories
afloat like mist at time's edges.
Its fiery tail wrote *genesis*
as it grazed the outer skin
of our earthly carapace,
pushed against ozone
layered like cake rings,

As it soars toward past lives unknown to us,
unknown to ancestors of ancestors,
it seeks tales of unformed planets,
rings of flame and gas,
dark holes where light bends,
constellations encrusted
with diamonds and dust.
We all want a peek into a looking glass
that will unfold like butterfly wings
to carry stories back to us like ancient griots
crossing deserts on camels,
armed with prayer rugs, cardamom tea, ghazals.

No one knows if ideas we spin about origins
will turn out prescient or useless.
No one knows what will be revealed or when.
No one knows what languages will be spoken.
Yesterday's mysteries will be unveiled
from a billion miles away.
Our own chronicles will unfurl,
told by prisms of light that will one day
bounce back from long dead stars,
flirting like fireflies as they spin, leap, dance.
We can almost hear them now,
whispering to us as lovers might.
This much is true: No memory will ever be quite the same.

Tales From a Weather Balloon

It was a beautiful week for a ride.
The skies were the blue of Spring robin's eggs.
The cumulus clouds were shape-shifting
over lush fields of golden wheat and rye.

Such lovely weather made it hard to hide.
Some warned that my weather mission begs
the motive question. Was I simply grifting
or something worse? Who would lie

about my purpose? I've flown far and wide
before without detection. Who pegs
me as a bad actor when I'm just drifting
overhead? How dare you charge me as a spy?

Yesterday I was happy just to glide
across the continent. Then—*Boom*—the dregs
of me scattered like confetti, sifting
down into the sea. Aren't you sad to say goodbye?

Examining Images From Space Telescopes

Everything we think we know now was understood
by arcs of diamond-crusted dust, rainbow-hued gasses
that have been travelling through the cosmos for millennia.
We stare at them now through origami lenses.

Arcs of diamond-crusted dust, rainbow-hued gasses
form luminous, lace-webbed, beaded necklaces.
We stare at them now through origami lenses—
a curtain of light that beckons us to examine shadows.

From a luminous, lace-webbed, beaded necklace
encircling the bodies of unnamed galaxies,
a curtain of light beckons us to examine shadows,
dissect the acrobatic movements of unknown star fields

that encircle the bodies of unnamed galaxies,
cavorting like aerialists across ancient colosseums.
We dissect the acrobatic movements of unknown star fields
where black holes beckon like impassioned lovers

cavorting like aerialists across ancient colosseums,
conjoined by flame and fury, ice and obscurity.
While black holes beckon like impassioned lovers,
our own galaxy sits, tiny as a viral lab droplet.

Conjoined by flame and fury, ice and obscurity,
we struggle to comprehend our fates and futures.
Our own galaxy sits, tiny as a viral lab droplet,
as we stare at swirls of wind and fire far past the Milky Way.

We must struggle to comprehend our fates and futures,
try to pierce walls so vast we cannot see the other side.
We see swirls of wind and fire engulf the Milky Way,
spiral past our control, perturbing space and time.

We hope to pierce walls so vast we cannot see the other side,
while we still have the luxury of time and intention,
before they spiral past our control to perturb space and time.
We can now fix our lenses on illumination,

while we still have the luxury of time and intention.
Everything we know now was understood long ago.
Illumined by origami lenses, we fix on knowledge
that has traveled through the cosmos for millennia.

Sestina For Light Dreams

Can we be both candle and its mirror image blaze?
Pound and Plato knew knowledge could be radiant.
To be like Illuminati, who sought enlightenment,
a philosophy professor formed *The Shining Path.*
Although firelight has its pulsing cone of darkness,
everyone wants to arrive at tunnel's ending light.

Buddha's last instruction: *Make of yourself a light.*
As long as we allow hope to remain ablaze—
where *only light can drive out darkness—*
we can become Martin Luther King, Jr.'s radiant
followers, marching along rebellion's petrous path,
in search of democracy's enlightenment.

A crack in everything: Leonard Cohen's enlightenment
on the hard travelling ways of light.
Wisest of the song poets, his resplendent path
can lead us from shadows. Once, my hopes ablaze
from teenaged angst, my mother urged radiance.
Let your light shine, she warned. *Darkness*

does not become you. Later on, darkness
was dissed by a shrink who said enlightenment
came from dragging every non-radiant
thought up to the surface to *shine a light
on it.* Then, strike a match. Let it blaze
until you are walking on a luminous path.

The Milky Way irradiates our cosmic path-
ways. Diamond mandalas dazzle against darkness,
as if ancient gods had transformed sky to a blaze
of glorious flames. We seek enlightenment
from mirrored lenses pointed into space. Einstein's light
has bent, looped, curved to make history radiant.

We want to study each starry memoir, radiant
with autobiographical detail. Track each path
backward to its origin story—an exploding light
from once-sleeping dreams that burned darkness
away, leaving behind hints of enlightenment
to float like sparks from a campfire's blaze.

Some nights that starlight is so vast, so radiant,
we cannot imagine its shadows could obscure our path
to enlightenment. We all seek comfort from that blaze.

Flight. Reimagined. II*

Coronas surround the globe.
Monarch butterflies delay their
returns, rest in jungle mists
to await news of normalcy.
Later, when it is deemed safer,
the flutter of their wings rumbles
across mountain ranges, echoes
in tide pools, mimics breathless waves.
They enter skies that have shed smoke
so they pass sights unknown to their
ancestors. Along the way, they meet
other gravity-defying travelers
who are shrugging off fears
of extinction like a second skin.
As they fly, a new sound emerges:
Innocence. Wishful thinking. Jubilation.
Inspiration for new symphonies.

*Notes on Selected Poems

"A Monarch Butterfly Poses Some Questions"

Monarch butterflies have just been placed on the endangered species list by the International Union for Conservation of Nature. Monarchs in North America have been in decline for many years. Wildlife surveys show Monarch population declines ranging from 84 to 99.9 percent over the past twenty to thirty years.

"Miracle Of The Honeybees"

In September 2021, the Cumbre Vieja volcano in the Canary Islands erupted, leaving great devastation in its wake. Six weeks later, a beekeeper returned to one of the devastated villages to assess the damage. He found five hives covered in volcanic ash. Inside, tens of thousands of Canary black bees, were still alive and buzzing. They had sealed themselves inside each hive using propolis to protect themselves from poisonous gases and consumed stored honey to keep from starving. Each secured hive contained one tiny pathway out but otherwise completely protected each colony.

"Night Witches"

The Soviet Union was the first country to officially engage women as combat fighters. Four hundred women, using faulty and second-hand equipment, served as pilots, navigators, maintenance and ground crew workers during World War II. Two-person crews flew as many as 18 nightly missions in planes that could carry only two bombs at a time. The Nazis called them "night witches" because they were almost undetectable other than a slight "whooshing" noise just before they dropped their bombs, a sound the Germans compared to that of a broom sweeping. Overall, they flew over 30,000 missions and lost only 30 pilots.

"Trying On The Wings Of Prayer"

On March 18, 2018, Sacramento police officers shot 23-year-old Stephon Clark 20 times as he stood unarmed in his grandmother's back yard. They were not prosecuted for the murder.

"Is Exodus The Same As Flight?"

Israel's Supreme Court recently declared that the Israeli military may clear a rural West Bank area known as Masafer Yatta for use as a live-fire military training ground. This will result in the expulsion of about 1,200 residents of thirteen Palestinian villages in the region, an act considered by the United Nations to be a violation of international law. Villagers say their families have lived in the region for generations. Many have been forced from their homes into caves in an effort to escape forced transfer from their ancestral lands. *New York Times,* October 23, 2022, p.A8.

"Escape Velocity"

In physics, escape velocity is the minimum speed needed for a free object to escape from the gravitational influence of a massive body. It is slower the further away from the body an object is, and slower for less massive bodies. The escape velocity from Earth's surface is about 11.186 km/s.

"Bird Watcher's Diary"

On May 25, 2020, Amy Cooper, a white woman walking her dog in The Ramble, a protected bird-watching area of New York City's Central Park, was asked by Christian Cooper, a seasoned birdwatcher, to leash her dog. She responded to his request by calling the police to falsely claim she was being "threatened" by a Black man. On the same day, in Minneapolis, Minnesota, George Floyd was murdered by the police. Both events were captured on telephone videos which went viral.

"Murmurations"

Murmuration is the name given to flocks of starlings flying together in coordinated, whirling, ever-changing patterns. Hundreds, even thousands, of these iridescent birds often look like shape-shifting clouds as they sweep across the skies. Flocks have no leaders and no pre-set plans for their flights. Instead, scientists believe that each bird communicates with its seven nearest neighbors as they move as a collective whole. Murmurations often occur in response to the presence of a predator such as a hawk or falcon.

"An Ordinary Day"

New York City's Hart Island has been the site of burials for the poor, the unknown, prisoners and stillborn babies since 1868. It is believed that more than one million bodies are buried there. During the COVID-19 pandemic, gravediggers often worked seven days a week burying victims whose families did not claim their bodies. *Washington Post,* "New York City's Family Tomb," April 27, 2020.

"Couples Counseling Advice From Great Horned Owls"

In New York, Great Horned Owls typically begin their mating season in December when the weather turns cold and blustery. The male owls are particularly loud during this time of year when they adopt various strategies to attract female partners for the breeding season ahead.

"In The Wind. I"

The U.S. Fish & Wildlife Service recently announced that 23 species had officially become extinct. Among them was the ivory-billed woodpecker, nicknamed "the Lord God bird" because people who saw it were said to exclaim "Lord God, what a bird!" Its last official sighting was in 1944, though unconfirmed sightings have been reported since then in the swamps of Arkansas, Louisiana, Mississippi and Florida. Wildlife experts blame the bird's demise on climate change, unchecked development, water pollution, logging, competition from invasive species and hunters. *Associated Press* September 29, 2021. A 2005 song by Sufjan Stevens, "The Lord God Bird," cautions bird watchers to "beware lest they see it fall."

"How To Tally Some Of Our Abundant Losses"

In September 2019, the journal *Science* released a study showing that birds numbers in the United States and Canada have decreased by twenty-nine percent since 1970, a number equivalent to almost three billion birds. The study evaluated more than 500 species and included birds typically thought to be unthreatened such as sparrows, blackbirds and robins. Many causes for the decline were identified, including loss of natural habitats to development and modern agriculture, pesticides and diminished protections for wilderness areas and wetlands. The National Audubon Society described the findings as a "full-blown crisis." Studies of birds in Europe have reached similar conclusions. *Washington Post,* September 20, 2019, A1

"La Clairvoyance"

René Magritte, the Belgian surrealist artist, painted many pictures with birds—caged, in flight, filled with clouds or stars or leaves, made of stone, wearing suits. In his 1936 painting, *La Clairvoyance,* Magritte's self-portrait captures an artist staring at his "model"—an unhatched bird's egg—while the painting on the canvas is of a fully-hatched and grown bird, leaving viewers to contemplate the ways one can predict one's future or mine the subconscious for artistic inspiration.

"Creating The Sounds Of Music"

Most songbirds produce sound using a unique, tiny vibrating organ known as a syrinx. Located at the top of the bird's windpipe, between trachea and bronchi, the syrinx uses almost all the air that passes through it, in contrast to humans who use only about two percent of the air exhaled through their larynx. Several pairs of muscles control the syrinx, allowing birds to produce multiple notes and trilling sounds.

"Who Can Hear A Love Song?"

The Moto braccatus, a Hawaiian songbird native to the island of Kauai, became extinct in the late 1980s, victim to climate change, development and pollution. The last female died in 1982. For five years after her death, the male continued to issue his mating call. It was recorded before he died. It can be heard at Bird Note: "Song of the Kauai O'o."

"Man Talking To Bird"

William "Bill" Traylor was a self-taught American artist who was born into slavery in Alabama in 1854. Traylor did not begin to draw until he was in his 80's. His paintings, often on cardboard or other basic materials, focused on simple human figures, animals or birds. He often used stark colors and dramatic shapes and patterns. Many works reflect the violence, racism and classism undoubtedly encountered during Traylor's life. Traylor's works are now sought after by museums and collectors but he was buried in a pauper's grave in 1949.

"The Future Of Civilization"

Dimitry Kokh, a Russian wildlife photographer, recently used a drone camera with low noise propellers to photograph polar bears living on Wrangel Island in Kolyuchin, a region near the northern coast of Chukotka in the Russian Federation. The bears have taken up residence in various outbuildings that once housed a weather station. Built in the 1930s, the station was abandoned by humans in 1992. Wrangel Island is a UNESCO-designated nature preserve and refuge.

"Cease Fire"

For more than a decade, the Syrian civil war has been the focus of more than 143 "cease fire" declarations. Most have focused on specific conflict zones. There has not been a country-wide cease fire declaration since 2016 when the United Nations, the United States and Russia negotiated one that lasted for nearly five months. Most declared cease fires held for very limited periods of time and were often declared by one side for purely tactical purposes such as re-arming or re-positioning troops, rather than for humanitarian purposes. Since 2016, most cessations of fighting have been negotiated by Russia or Turkey or unilaterally declared by President Assad for tactical reasons.

"Observing The Passage Of Venus"

In early April 2020 at the height of the first wave of COVID-19, Venus became most brilliant as she traveled closest to Earth, wandering across the Pleiades star cluster to enter the arc of the Zodiac.

"Ode To Companionship"

Astronomers recently announced discovery of the gas phosphine (PH3) in the upper cloud deck atmosphere of Venus, Earth's closest neighboring planet. Phosphine is considered a "biosignature" of life. Its discovery suggests that oceans might once have existed on Venus. Further study could show whether Venus was once habitable and/or whether our definitions of "life" might vary.

"Exploring The Limits Of Curiosity"

NASA's Mars Rover, Curiosity, has successfully drilled into rock slabs which are believed to be formed from sediment from ancient streams or lakes. Material from these holes was used for two "wet chemistry" experiments that extracted organic molecules preserved in the rock. The results suggest that ancient Mars was habitable and capable of supporting life.

"When Hope Is The Thing We Want To Convey"

The Golden Shovel poetry form was invented by Terrance Hayes in homage to the poet Gwendolyn Brooks. Based on her poem, "We Real Cool," Hayes wrote "The Golden Shovel" in 2010, using each word in the poem's original lines as the last word in his own poem. Since then, the form has undergone many refinements, including use of poems by authors other than Brooks. In 2019, Hayes edited "The Golden Shovel Anthology," a collection of works by many poets using the form.

"Cloud Cover"

On May 24, 2022, an 18-year-old armed with an assault weapon killed 19 schoolchildren and two teachers at Robb Elementary School in Uvalde, Texas. Seventeen more were grievously injured. The killings occurred ten days after a racially motivated mass murder at a Buffalo, NY supermarket. Despite outrage and calls to ban assault rifles and other deadly weapons, nothing of any significance has occurred to prevent more such attacks. In the first six months of 2023, over 360 mass shootings took place in the United States.

"Villanelle For Black Holes"

In May 2022, "Event Horizon Telescope," a collaboration of hundreds of astronomers from eighty institutions, released the first photograph of the largest black hole yet to be observed by humans. "Sagittarius A" is located 26,000 miles from earth in the center of the Milky Way galaxy. Although black holes are normally not visible because light cannot travel fast enough to escape being sucked into their vortex, images sent by eight linked satellite radio dishes revealed a giant black shadow surrounded by swirling gas and other debris that glows brightly around it.

Statistics maintained by Gun Violence Archive revealed that there were 648 mass shootings in the United States for calendar year 2022 (defined as an event where at least four people are killed, not including the shooter). At least 20,101 people were killed by guns and another 38,448 were injured. The Switzerland-based "Small Arms Survey" estimates that there are 393 million firearms in the United States, outnumbering our population of about 334 million. Gun violence is now the leading cause of children's deaths in the United States.

"Flight. Reimagined. II"

By May 2020, the COVID pandemic had led to significantly reduced air pollution as fossil fuel-driven transportation such as airlines, automobiles, trucks, trains and other climate-change impacting vehicles largely reduced their carbon footprint. Photographs of earth taken from space shuttles and satellites were remarkably clear and sharp with heightened color and detail.

About the Author

Mary K. O'Melveny lives near Woodstock, New York with her wife Susan. After retiring from a distinguished career as a labor rights attorney, Mary revisited poetry writing, an interest dating back to her college days. Mary's poetry has been published in many print and on-line literary journals, including *Aji Poetry Magazine, Allegro Poetry Magazine, ArielChart, Auroras and Blossoms, Beltway Poetry Quarterly, Coastal Shelf, FLARE: The Flagler Review In Layman's Terms, Into The Void, Light Journal, Lightwood, Jerry Jazz Musician, Jewish Currents, Minerva Rising, Passager Literary Journal, Slippery Elm Literary Journal, Split Rock Review, Songs of Eretz Poetry Review, The Global Poemic, New Reader, The Offbeat, The Poet's Billow, The Raven's Perch, The Voices Project, The Write Place at the Write Time, THINK, Twisted Vine Literary Journal, V Literary Journal, Voice of Eve, West Texas Review,* and *Workers Write.*

Mary's poems have also appeared in anthologies, including *American Writer's Review* (San Fedele Press), *Borders and Boundaries, Essential Voices: A COVID-19 Anthology, Kingdoms In The Wild, The Four Freedoms* (Shanti Arts), *Awake in the World, Volume II* (Riverfeet Press), *Poems From the Lockdown* (Willowdown Books), *Poems of Political Protest* (City Limits). National blog sites such as *The New Verse News* and *Writing In A Woman's Voice* have also published many of Mary's poems.

Mary is an active member of several writing organizations, including *The Hudson Valley Women's Writing Group.* Her poetry appears in two anthologies of works by members of that group: *An Apple In Her Hand* (Codhill Press, 2019) and *Rethinking The Ground Rules* (Mediacs Books, 2022). Mary is the author of the poetry chapbook *A Woman of a Certain Age* (Finishing Line Press, 2018) and two poetry collections: *Merging Star Hypotheses* (Finishing Line Press, 2020) and *Dispatches From The Memory Care Museum* (Kelsay Books, 2021). Mary's poetry has received award recognition in national and international poetry contests and has been nominated for a Pushcart Prize. The author's collection *Merging Star Hypotheses* was a semi-finalist for the 2019 Washington Prize sponsored by The Word Works. She won First Place in the 2017 Raynes Poetry Competition, the 2019 Slippery Elm Literary Journal Poetry Prize and the 2020 Poems of Political Protest Competition sponsored by City Limits Publishing.

She was a "Highly Commended" Finalist for the 2020 Anthology Magazine Poetry Prize and a Finalist, Semi-Finalist or Honorable Mention award winner in poetry competitions sponsored by *The Poet's Billow* (Pangaea Prize; Atlantis Award), *Winning Writers* (Tom Howard/Margaret Reid Poetry Competition) and *Writer's Digest,* among others.

Award-winning poems in this volume include "Cease Fire" (First Prize, 2017 Raynes Poetry Competition), "Escape Velocity" (Finalist, 2019 Tom Howard/Margaret Reid Poetry Competition sponsored by *Winning Writers*), and "Villanelle For Black Holes" (Finalist, 2023 *Slippery Elm Literary Journal* Poetry Competition).

Mary's website is:
www.marykomelvenypoet.com

www.ingramcontent.com/pod-product-compliance
Lightning Source LLC
Chambersburg PA
CBHW022013160426
43197CB00007B/414